Redis Essentials

Harness the power of Redis to integrate and manage your projects efficiently

Maxwell Dayvson Da Silva

Hugo Lopes Tavares

BIRMINGHAM - MUMBAI

Redis Essentials

First published: September 2015

Production reference: 1030915

Published by Packt Publishing Ltd.
Livery Place
35 Livery Street
Birmingham B3 2PB, UK.

ISBN 978-1-78439-245-1

www.packtpub.com

Credits

Authors
  Maxwell Dayvson Da Silva
  Hugo Lopes Tavares

Reviewers
  Gustavo Franco
  Chad Lung
  Stephen McDonald
  Yi Wang

Commissioning Editor
  Sarah Crofton

Acquisition Editor
  Harsha Bharwani

Content Development Editor
  Kirti Patil

Technical Editor
  Menza Mathew

Copy Editor
  Vikrant Phadkay

Project Coordinator
  Nidhi Joshi

Proofreader
  Safis Editing

Indexer
  Rekha Nair

Production Coordinator
  Manu Joseph

Cover Work
  Manu Joseph

Cover Image
  Renata Pereira Rocha Moreira

About the Authors

Maxwell Dayvson Da Silva, a self-taught programmer, is the director of technology at The New York Times.

Born in Recife, Brazil, he is a video specialist and is most interested in bringing technology to a global audience. His work has ranged from developing and delivering highly scalable products to innovating and implementing large-scale video solutions. Prior to joining the Times, he worked for Globo, Brazil's leading media network, and Terra, a global digital media company.

Additionally, he has spoken at conferences such as Campus Party, FISL, SET Broadcast and Cable, Streaming Media East, and Streaming Media West. Maxwell has also devoted time to speaking at several Brazilian universities, including UFGRS, IFRS, UDESC, and FEEVALE-RS.

He is a contributor to and creator of some open source projects. You can find them at `https://github.com/dayvson`. Outside of his professional work, Maxwell regularly combines his passion for art and science to create games and interactive art installations. His son, Arthur, inspires him to seek opportunities to bring science into the lives of young people, both in New York and abroad.

Although *Redis Essentials* is Maxwell's first book, he has done technical reviewing for two others, *Extending Bootstrap* and *Learning JavaScript Data Structures and Algorithms*. You can contact him on LinkedIn at `http://www.linkedin.com/in/dayvson`.

Hugo Lopes Tavares is a software developer from Brazil who currently works as a platform engineer at Yipit, a technology company focused on data aggregation and analysis. Prior to his work in the United States, Hugo worked on live streaming video development for Globo.com, the Internet branch of Grupo Globo, which is the largest media conglomerate in Latin America.

Having been involved in open source software, he has made a significant impact in this field. He was a main contributor to pip (the Python package installer), wrote improvements to CPython and the Python standard library, coauthored Splinter (a web-testing tool), and contributed to many well-known projects. Some of his contributions can be found at https://github.com/hltbra.

Additionally, Hugo worked at NSI (Information Systems Research Group), carrying out research and development on agile methods and software quality for the Brazilian government. Within his research, he created some testing tools, the most famous of which are Should-DSL and PyCukes, which are mentioned in *Python Testing Cookbook, Packt Publishing* (Should-DSL has its own section in it).

When Hugo is not doing anything related to technology, he is involved in strength training as an amateur powerlifter.

You can contact him on LinkedIn at https://www.linkedin.com/in/hltbra.

Acknowledgments

I would like to express my gratitude for my amazing and supportive partner in crime and life, Karalyn Lathrop (a.k.a. KC). She was incredibly supportive and helpful in the making of this book in so many ways that I cannot describe how thankful I am for her.

I am incredibly grateful to my son, Arthur, for being so amazingly sweet and funny. Also, thanks to him for making my life so much better, even with the long distance that keeps us far way.

There are many people I'm thankful to for the making of this book: my mom, Mauriceia, for all the love that she has given me! My aunt, Maristela, for all the support and advice; the sweetest grandmothers, Alderita and Fran Kozina; and Juliane, for being a supermom and taking care of our son when I am far way.

I give thanks to Nina Feinberg. Her help in this project was fundamental in improving the quality of the writing and consistency of this book.

Also, I would like to give special acknowledgements to the many friends and colleagues who helped me during this journey. Each one of you made a significant contribution to this project, and I am so thankful: Lincoln Clarete, Cristian Taveras, Deep Kapadia, Flavio Ribeiro, Jose Muanis, Kentaro Kaji, Michael Sarullo, Manu Menezes, Gustavo Franco, and Renata Tavares.

Finally, I give my huge thanks to Hugo Tavares for sharing this crazy experience with me. I'm honoured that he accepted my invite. Writing this book was challenging, exciting, and rewarding in so many ways. I had a lot of fun and learned a lot during the process. It's been an honour and privilege working with you.

– Maxwell Dayvson Da Silva

I would like to thank my wife, Renata, for all her support and for designing a beautiful cover for this book. This project would not have succeeded without her support. Thanks, my love!

I also thank my parents, Paulo and Maria das Graças, for always loving me, supporting my education and all my decisions, and giving me good advice on life.

I am very thankful to Karalyn Lathrop and Nina Feinberg, who reviewed this book, and the technical reviewers. They improved this book's quality a lot.

I also thank Maxwell Dayvson for inviting me to join him to write this great book. It has been an amazing experience, and I learned a lot by working with him. Thanks, my friend! I am very proud of both of us.

– Hugo Lopes Tavares

About the Reviewers

Gustavo Franco is a tech lead manager for site reliability engineering at Google. He has worked on cloud platforms, social media, and several other services. He has also been a Debian developer for more than 10 years. His career spans over 13 years of DevOps-related work, including a FIFA World Cup online broadcast, migrating several Google internal systems to Goobuntu, the Google Compute Engine launch, and more.

Chad Lung is a cloud engineer in the EMC Rubicon cloud services group. Currently, he is an active OpenStack contributor and has over 18 years of industry experience in various roles.

Originally born in Canada, he moved to the United States in 1997 and began his software engineering career with full force. He has worked with various technologies and for large cloud-based companies, such as Rackspace and EMC.

Chad has three sons and lives with his wife in San Antonio, Texas, USA.

Stephen McDonald is a software engineer from Sydney, Australia. He currently works for Google. He is also the creator of various Redis-related open source projects, such as the hot-redis client library for Python, and CurioDB, a distributed-by-default clone of Redis that has been built with Scala and Akka. You can visit `http://jupo.org` for more information about him.

Yi Wang is currently a lead software engineer at Trendalytics, a fashion tech start-up. He is responsible for specifying, designing, and implementing data collection, visualization, and analysis pipelines on cloud platforms. He has over 8 years of data analytics and visualization experience at enterprises and start-ups such as Opera Solutions (big data), Maxifier (advertising technology), Sapient Global Markets, and Microsoft Research Asia. He holds a master's degree in computer science from Columbia University and a master's degree in physics from Peking University, with a mixed academic background in math, chemistry, and biology.

I must thank my wife, Jingjing, and my kids, Aria and Alan, for all the support.

www.PacktPub.com

Support files, eBooks, discount offers, and more

For support files and downloads related to your book, please visit www.PacktPub.com.

Did you know that Packt offers eBook versions of every book published, with PDF and ePub files available? You can upgrade to the eBook version at www.PacktPub.com and as a print book customer, you are entitled to a discount on the eBook copy. Get in touch with us at service@packtpub.com for more details.

At www.PacktPub.com, you can also read a collection of free technical articles, sign up for a range of free newsletters and receive exclusive discounts and offers on Packt books and eBooks.

https://www2.packtpub.com/books/subscription/packtlib

Do you need instant solutions to your IT questions? PacktLib is Packt's online digital book library. Here, you can search, access, and read Packt's entire library of books.

Why subscribe?

- Fully searchable across every book published by Packt
- Copy and paste, print, and bookmark content
- On demand and accessible via a web browser

Free access for Packt account holders

If you have an account with Packt at www.PacktPub.com, you can use this to access PacktLib today and view 9 entirely free books. Simply use your login credentials for immediate access.

Table of Contents

Preface

Redis is the most popular in-memory key-value data store. It is very lightweight and its data types give it an edge over other competitors. If you need an in-memory database or a high-performance cache system that is simple to use and highly scalable, Redis is what you should use.

This book is a fast-paced guide that teaches you the fundamentals of data types, explains how to manage data through commands, and shares experiences from big players in the industry.

What this book covers

Chapter 1, Getting Started (The Baby Steps), shows you how to install Redis and how to use **redis-cli**, the default Redis command-line interface. It also shows you how to install Node.js and goes through a quick JavaScript syntax reference. The String, List, and Hash data types are covered in detail, along with examples of **redis-cli** and Node.js.

Chapter 2, Advanced Data Types (Earning a Black Belt), is a continuation of the previous chapter. It presents the Set, Sorted Set, Bitmap, and HyperLogLog data types. All the examples here are implemented with **redis-cli** and Node.js.

Chapter 3, Time Series (A Collection of Observations), uses all of the knowledge of data types from the previous chapters to build a time series library in Node.js. The examples are incremental; the library is initially implemented using the String data type, and then the solution is improved and optimized by using the Hash data type. Uniqueness support is added to the String and Hash implementations by using the Sorted Set and HyperLogLog data types, respectively.

Chapter 4, Commands (Where the Wild Things Are), introduces Pub/Sub, transactions, and pipelines. It also introduces the scripting mechanism, which uses the Lua programming language to extend Redis. A quick Lua syntax reference is also presented. A great variety of Redis commands are presented in this chapter, including the administration commands and data type commands that were not covered in the previous chapters. This chapter also shows you how to change Redis's configuration to optimize different data types for memory or performance.

Chapter 5, Clients for Your Favorite Language (Become a Redis Polyglot), shows how to use Redis with PHP, Python, and Ruby. This chapter highlights the features that vary more frequently with clients in different languages: blocking commands, transactions, pipelines, and scripting.

Chapter 6, Common Pitfalls (Avoiding Traps), illustrates some common mistakes when using Redis in a production environment and related stories from real-world companies. The pitfalls in this chapter include using the wrong data type for a given problem, using too much swap space, and using inefficient backup strategies.

Chapter 7, Security Techniques (Guard Your Data), shows how to set up basic security with Redis, disable and obfuscate commands, protect Redis with firewall rules, and use client-to-server SSL encryption with stunnel.

Chapter 8, Scaling Redis (Beyond a Single Instance), introduces RDB and AOF persistence, replication via Redis slaves, and different methods of partitioning data across different hosts. This chapter also shows how to use twemproxy to distribute Redis data across different instances transparently.

Chapter 9, Redis Cluster and Redis Sentinel (Collective Intelligence), demonstrates the differences between Redis Cluster and Redis Sentinel, their goals, and how they fit into the CAP theorem. It also shows how to set up both Sentinel and Cluster, their configurations, and what happens in different failure scenarios. Redis Cluster is covered in more detail, since it is more complex and has different tools for managing a cluster of instances. Cluster administration is explained via native Redis commands and the **redis-trib** tool.

What you need for this book

The examples in this book assume that you have a computer with GNU/Linux or Mac OS X. We also assume that the following are installed:

- Node.js 0.12.4
- NPM
- Redis 3.X

The following requirements are optional when using other Redis clients:

- Python 2.7
- pip
- Ruby 1.9+
- RubyGems
- PHP 5.5+
- Composer

Who this book is for

This book is intended for those with or without previous experience who want to learn about Redis. Using examples of real-world applications, this book shows problems solved by companies who have been using Redis for years.

Providing a foundation for an understanding of the capabilities of Redis, this book will teach you how to extend and scale Redis in real-life situations.

Conventions

In this book, you will find a number of text styles that distinguish between different kinds of information. Here are some examples of these styles and an explanation of their meaning.

A block of code is set as follows:

```
var redis = require("redis"); // 1
var client = redis.createClient(); // 2
```

When we wish to draw your attention to a particular part of a code block, the relevant lines or items are set in bold:

```
var redis = require("redis"); // 1
var client = redis.createClient(); // 2
console.log("Redis Essentials"); // 3
```

Please note that all the code snippets in this book will have inline comments with numbers. After the code is presented, it will be explained by referencing those numbers.

Each command line starts with a dollar sign ($):

```
$ redis-server
```

The following conventions are used in this book for **redis-cli**:

- Commands are written in bold uppercase letters (**SET**).
- Keys are written in italicized lowercase letters (**GET** *mykey*).
- Values are written without any text formatting (**SET** *mykey* "my value").

```
$ redis-cli
127.0.0.1:6379> SET mykey "my value"
```

In this book, all filenames, function names, and variable names are written in italics. Examples:

- Create a file called *my-filename.js*.
- Execute the function *myFunctionName*.
- Create a variable called *myVariableName*.

All data types will be shown with the first letter capitalized (for example, Strings, Lists, Bitmaps, Sets, Sorted Sets, and HyperLogLogs) so that we can distinguish between a Redis data type and another existing term.

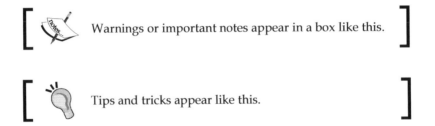

Warnings or important notes appear in a box like this.

Tips and tricks appear like this.

Reader feedback

Feedback from our readers is always welcome. Let's know what you think about this book—what you liked or disliked. Reader feedback is important for us as it helps us develop titles that you will really get the most out of.

To send us general feedback, simply e-mail feedback@packtpub.com, and mention the book's title in the subject of your message.

If there is a topic that you have expertise in and you are interested in either writing or contributing to a book, see our author guide at www.packtpub.com/authors.

Customer support

Now that you are the proud owner of a Packt book, we have a number of things to help you to get the most from your purchase.

Downloading the example code

You can download the example code files from your account at http://www.packtpub.com for all the Packt Publishing books you have purchased. If you purchased this book elsewhere, you can visit http://www.packtpub.com/support and register to have the files e-mailed directly to you.

All the code files from this book can be downloaded from GitHub as well: https://github.com/redis-essentials/book.

Errata

Although we have taken every care to ensure the accuracy of our content, mistakes do happen. If you find a mistake in one of our books—maybe a mistake in the text or the code—we would be grateful if you could report this to us. By doing so, you can save other readers from frustration and help us improve subsequent versions of this book. If you find any errata, please report them by visiting http://www.packtpub.com/submit-errata, selecting your book, clicking on the **Errata Submission Form** link, and entering the details of your errata. Once your errata are verified, your submission will be accepted and the errata will be uploaded to our website or added to any list of existing errata under the Errata section of that title.

To view the previously submitted errata, go to https://www.packtpub.com/books/content/support and enter the name of the book in the search field. The required information will appear under the **Errata** section.

Piracy

Piracy of copyrighted material on the Internet is an ongoing problem across all media. At Packt, we take the protection of our copyright and licenses very seriously. If you come across any illegal copies of our works in any form on the Internet, please provide us with the location address or website name immediately so that we can pursue a remedy.

Please contact us at copyright@packtpub.com with a link to the suspected pirated material.

We appreciate your help in protecting our authors and our ability to bring you valuable content.

Questions

If you have a problem with any aspect of this book, you can contact us at
questions@packtpub.com, and we will do our best to address the problem.

1
Getting Started
(The Baby Steps)

Redis is a NoSQL (Not only SQL) advanced key-value data store. It is also referred to as a data structure server because of its powerful data types, such as Strings, Hashes, Lists, Sets, Sorted Sets, Bitmaps, and HyperLogLogs. By default, Redis saves all data in the memory, therefore read and write operations are very fast. It can also cause data to persist in the disk. Data persistence in Redis can be achieved by creating a binary snapshot of the stored data or a human-readable file with a sequence of all executed commands over time. These are respectively known as snapshotting and journaling.

Additionally, Redis includes configurable key expiration, transactions, and publish/subscribe features. It also provides Lua scripting to extend Redis to create new commands. Combined, these features transform Redis into the Swiss Army knife of data type storage.

Redis stands for **REmote DIctionary Server**. It was written in C by *Salvatore Sanfilippo* in 2006 and currently has many contributors. There are Redis clients available for over 30 programming languages. The open source project can be found at `https://github.com/antirez/redis`. The official Redis documentation is also a really good resource of knowledge and can be found at `http://redis.io`.

Redis is a well-established open source project and has been used in production for years by big companies, including Twitter, GitHub, Tumblr, Pinterest, Instagram, Hulu, Flickr, and The New York Times.

This chapter is going to show you how to install Redis, introduce the command-line interface, introduce a Node.js client for Redis, and then present three data types in detail: Strings, Lists, and Hashes.

Redis data types are a very extensive subject. There is enough information to write a book that just describes how they work. We will present the most relevant and useful commands for each data type along with real-life use cases in the first two chapters. *Chapter 2, Advanced Data Types (Earning a Black Belt)*, is going to cover other data types: Sets, Sorted Sets, Bitmaps, and HyperLogLogs. After this chapter and the next have explained all data types, *Chapter 3, Time Series (A Collection of Observations)*, will present a time series implementation that uses multiple data types.

> Please note that all data types will be shown with the first letter capitalized (for example, Strings, Lists, Bitmaps, Sets, Sorted Sets, and HyperLogLogs) so that we can distinguish between a Redis data type and other existing terms.

Installation

At the time of writing this book, the stable version of Redis was 3.0. All examples presented in this book will work with this version, but it is very likely that newer versions of Redis are going to work as well. Redis is very strict in terms of backward compatibility, so it provides API stability between minor versions. We recommend that you install the latest version of Redis to get the recent bug fixes and performance improvements. Most of the content in this book will remain useful even if you work with a more recent version.

Officially, Redis can be compiled and used on Linux, OS X, OpenBSD, NetBSD, and FreeBSD.

Redis is not officially supported on Windows. However, the Microsoft Open Tech group develops and maintains a Windows port targeting Win64 architecture, which can be found at `https://github.com/MSOpenTech/redis`. We are not going to cover Windows installation or guarantee that the examples presented in this book will work on Windows.

Installing from source

The first thing we need to do is open a terminal and run the following commands to download and install Redis. The following commands can be executed in any *nix operating system (Ubuntu, CentOS, Debian, OS X, and so on). Some build tools are required to build Redis from source (for example, *gcc*, *make*, and so on). On Ubuntu and Debian, these tools can be installed by the package *build-essentials*.

On OS X, you will need *Xcode* and *Command Line Tools Package* installed. After the required build tools are installed, open a terminal window and execute the following commands:

```
$ curl -O http://download.redis.io/releases/redis-3.0.2.tar.gz
$ tar xzvf redis-3.0.2.tar.gz
$ cd redis-3.0.2
$ sudo make install
```

Every time you see a dollar sign ($) at the beginning of a code block, it means we are executing the command in a terminal window.

> Another way to install Redis is by using package managers, such as *yum*, *apt*, or *brew*. Make sure your package manager has Redis 3.0 or later available.

Hello Redis (command-line interface examples)

Redis comes with several executables. In this section, we are going to focus on **redis-server** and **redis-cli**.

redis-server is the actual Redis data store. It can be started in standalone mode or in cluster mode. For now, we are only going to use the single-instance mode and later (in *Chapter 9, Redis Cluster and Redis Sentinel (Collective Intelligence)*) we will cover cluster mode.

redis-cli is a command-line interface that can perform any Redis command (it is a Redis client). It makes learning to execute commands in Redis more intuitive.

This chapter is also going to introduce a Node.js client, and later (in *Chapter 5, Clients for Your Favorite Language (Become a Redis Polyglot)*) we will see how to use Redis with PHP, Python, and Ruby clients.

By default, Redis binds to port 6379, runs in standalone mode, and can be started with this line:

```
$ redis-server
```

Since no configuration was specified in this example, Redis will use default configurations.

It will output its PID (process ID) and the port that the clients should connect to, which is *6379* by default.

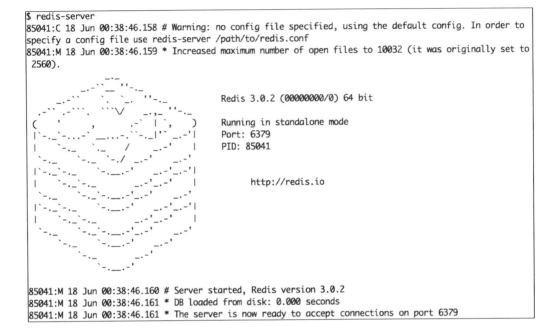

```
$ redis-server
85041:C 18 Jun 00:38:46.158 # Warning: no config file specified, using the default config. In order to
specify a config file use redis-server /path/to/redis.conf
85041:M 18 Jun 00:38:46.159 * Increased maximum number of open files to 10032 (it was originally set to
 2560).
```

```
                                        Redis 3.0.2 (00000000/0) 64 bit

                                        Running in standalone mode
                                        Port: 6379
                                        PID: 85041


                                            http://redis.io
```

```
85041:M 18 Jun 00:38:46.160 # Server started, Redis version 3.0.2
85041:M 18 Jun 00:38:46.161 * DB loaded from disk: 0.000 seconds
85041:M 18 Jun 00:38:46.161 * The server is now ready to accept connections on port 6379
```

Important note:

The following conventions will be used in this book for **redis-cli**:

- Commands are written in bold, uppercase letters (**SET**).
- Keys are written in italicized, lowercase letters (**GET** *mykey*).
- Values are written without any text formatting (**SET** *mykey* "my value").

The next snippet shows how to connect to the Redis server using **redis-cli**. Once connected, we use the **SET** command to create a key with a string value and then the **GET** command to read the key value:

```
$ redis-cli
127.0.0.1:6379> SET philosopher "socrates"
OK
127.0.0.1:6379> GET philosopher
"socrates"
127.0.0.1:6379>
```

The **HELP** command is useful for learning about command syntax. It displays the command parameters with a summary and examples. See the following example:

```
$ redis-cli
127.0.0.1:6379> HELP SET

  SET key value [EX seconds] [PX milliseconds] [NX|XX]
  summary: Set the string value of a key
  since: 1.0.0
  group: string
```

The **KEYS** command is also useful, as it returns all stored keys that match a pattern (it is a glob-style pattern, like the Unix shell glob pattern). In the following code, all stored key names that start with the letter "p" are returned:

```
$ redis-cli
127.0.0.1:6379> KEYS p*
1) "philosopher"
```

The **redis-cli** is a great tool for debugging and testing commands, but making real examples and applications using **redis-cli** is impractical. This book is going to use the JavaScript language and Node.js to support examples and explanations. We chose JavaScript because of its current popularity. The Node.js website (https://nodejs. org) provides binaries for Mac OS X, Windows, and Linux, which makes installation of Node.js really simple. Keep in mind that this is not a JavaScript book; we are going to use basic features of the language in our examples. If you do not know how to code in JavaScript, do not worry. A quick syntax reference is presented, and it should be enough to understand all the examples in this book.

 You can reproduce all the samples presented here in your favorite language. Redis will produce the same results regardless of the programming language.

Installing Node.js

Download and install Node.js from its website using the available binary packages. At the time of writing this book, the latest version of Node.js was 0.12.4. All examples are guaranteed to work with this version.

Node.js comes with a package manager called **Node Package Manager (NPM)**, which is responsible for managing and installing all Node.js dependencies and libraries. Think of it as **pip** for Python or **cpan** for Perl.

We recommend that you create a folder called *redis-essentials* to save all the files and libraries necessary for running the examples. We also recommend that you create one folder for each chapter of this book for organization purposes.

All Node.js examples in this book require the library *redis*, which can be installed with NPM:

```
$ cd redis-essentials
$ npm install redis
```

NPM will create a folder called *node_modules*. This is where the *redis* client is installed.

JavaScript syntax quick reference guide

If you know the basics of JavaScript, you can skip this section. Here is a quick overview of JavaScript:

- Use the keyword **var** to define a variable:

  ```
  var myAge = 31;
  ```

- Use // for inline comments and /* */ for multiline comments:

  ```
  // this is an inline comment
  /* this
  is a
  multi-line
  comment
  */
  ```

- Conditional statements:

  ```
  if (myAge > 29) {
    console.log("I am not in my twenties anymore!");
  } else {
    console.log("I am still in my twenties!");
  }
  ```

- Defining a function:

  ```
  function nameOfMyFunction(argument1, argument2) {
    console.log(argument1, argument2);
  }
  ```

- Executing a function:

  ```
  nameOfMyFunction("First Value", "Second Value");
  ```

- A function can also behave as a class and have methods, properties, and instances. Properties are accessed through the keyword **this**:

```
function Car(maxSpeed) {
  this.maxSpeed = maxSpeed;
  this.currentSpeed = 0;
}
```

- The standard way to create a prototyped method for a function in JavaScript is by using the property *prototype*:

```
Car.prototype.brake = function() {
  if (this.currentSpeed > 0) {
    this.currentSpeed -= 5;
  }
};


Car.prototype.accelerate = function() {
  if (this.currentSpeed < this.maxSpeed) {
    this.currentSpeed += 5;
  }
};
```

- To create an instance of a class in JavaScript, use the keyword *new*:

```
var car = new Car(100);
car.accelerate();
car.accelerate();
car.brake();
```

- Arrays and objects:

```
var myArray = [];
var myObject = {};
```

- Callbacks in JavaScript:

```
var friends = ["Karalyn", "Patrik", "Bernardo"];
friends.forEach(function (name, index) {
  console.log(index + 1, name); // 1 Karalyn, 2 Patrik, 3 Bernardo
});
```

A callback in this example is an anonymous function that is passed to another function as a parameter, so it is called (or executed) inside the other function. As you can see in the preceding example, the *forEach* array method expects a callback function. It executes the provided callback once for each element in the array. It is very common to find asynchronous functions/methods that expect callbacks in JavaScript.

If you want to know more about JavaScript syntax and features, we recommend the Mozilla Developer Network website at `https://developer.mozilla.org/en-US/docs/Web/JavaScript`.

Hello World with Node.js and Redis

This section shows the basics of creating a JavaScript program using Redis. It is important to understand this foundation since the upcoming examples use the same principles.

> In this book, all filenames, function names, and variable names are italicized. Some sentences follow this convention:
> - Create a file called *my-filename.js*.
> - Execute the function *myFunctionName*.
> - Create a variable called *myVariableName*.

Create a file called *hello.js* with the following code:

```
var redis = require("redis"); // 1
var client = redis.createClient(); // 2
client.set("my_key", "Hello World using Node.js and Redis"); // 3
client.get("my_key", redis.print); // 4
client.quit(); // 5
```

> Please note that all the code snippets in this book will have inline comments with numbers. After the code is presented, it will be explained by referencing those numbers.

1. Require the *redis* library in Node.js. This is equivalent to *import* in Go, Python, or Java.

2. Create the Redis client object.

3. Execute the Redis command **SET** to save a String in a key called *my_key*.

4. Execute the Redis command **GET** to get the value stored in *my_key*, and then output it.

5. Close the connection with the Redis server.

> Lines **1**, **2**, and **5** of this example will be used in the majority of the examples that use Node.js.

Run *hello.js* with the *node* command (*node* is the Node.js interpreter):

```
$ node hello.js
Reply: Hello World using Node.js and Redis
```

Redis data types

After you have understood how Redis data types work, you will be able to design better applications and make better use of the available resources. It will also help you decide whether Redis is the right solution for your problem. The main reason for Redis to have many data types is very simple: one size does not fit all, and different problems require different solutions.

Although you do not need to use all the data types, it is important to understand how they work so that you can choose the right ones. By the end of this book, you will have a full understanding of these data types and know how to improve the performance of your applications using Redis.

Strings

Strings are the most versatile data types in Redis because they have many commands and multiple purposes. A String can behave as an integer, float, text string, or bitmap based on its value and the commands used. It can store any kind of data: text (XML, JSON, HTML, or raw text), integers, floats, or binary data (videos, images, or audio files). A String value cannot exceed 512 MB of text or binary data.

The following are some use cases for Strings:

- **Cache mechanisms**: It is possible to cache text or binary data in Redis, which could be anything from HTML pages and API responses to images and videos. A simple cache system can be implemented with the commands **SET**, **GET**, **MSET**, and **MGET**.

- **Cache with automatic expiration**: Strings combined with automatic key expiration can make a robust cache system using the commands **SETEX**, **EXPIRE**, and **EXPIREAT**. This is very useful when database queries take a long time to run and can be cached for a given period of time. Consequently, this avoids running those queries too frequently and can give a performance boost to applications.

- **Counting**: A counter can easily be implemented with Strings and the commands **INCR** and **INCRBY**. Good examples of counters are page views, video views, and likes. Strings also provide other counting commands, such as **DECR**, **DECRBY**, and **INCRFLOATBY**.

String examples with redis-cli

The **MSET** command sets the values of multiple keys at once. The arguments are key-value pairs separated by spaces.

The **MGET** command retrieves the values of multiple key names at once, and the key names are separated by spaces.

The following is a combined example for the preceding commands:

```
$ redis-cli
127.0.0.1:6379> MSET first "First Key value" second "Second Key value"
OK
127.0.0.1:6379> MGET first second
1) "First Key value"
2) "Second Key value"
```

The **EXPIRE** command adds an expiration time (in seconds) to a given key. After that time, the key is automatically deleted. It returns *1* if the expiration is set successfully and *0* if the key does not exist or cannot be set.

The **TTL (Time To Live)** command returns one of the following:

- **A positive integer**: This is the amount of seconds a given key has left to live
- **-2**: If the key is expired or does not exist
- **-1**: If the key exists but has no expiration time set

```
$ redis-cli
127.0.0.1:6379> SET current_chapter "Chapter 1"
OK
127.0.0.1:6379> EXPIRE current_chapter 10
(integer) 1
127.0.0.1:6379> GET current_chapter
"Chapter 1"
127.0.0.1:6379> TTL current_chapter
(integer) 3
127.0.0.1:6379> TTL current_chapter
```

```
(integer) -2
127.0.0.1:6379> GET current_chapter
(nil)
127.0.0.1:6379>
```

The commands **INCR** and **INCRBY** have very similar functionality. **INCR** increments a key by *1* and returns the incremented value, whereas **INCRBY** increments a key by the given integer and returns the incremented value. **DECR** and **DECRBY** are the opposites of **INCR** and **INCRBY**. The only difference is that **DECR** and **DECRBY** decrements a key.

The command **INCRBYFLOAT** increments a key by a given float number and returns the new value. **INCRBY**, **DECRBY**, and **INCRBYFLOAT** accept either a positive or a negative number:

```
$ redis-cli
127.0.0.1:6379> SET counter 100
OK
127.0.0.1:6379> INCR counter
(integer) 101
127.0.0.1:6379> INCRBY counter 5
(integer) 106
127.0.0.1:6379> DECR counter
(integer) 105
127.0.0.1:6379> DECRBY counter 100
(integer) 5
127.0.0.1:6379> GET counter
"5"
127.0.0.1:6379> INCRBYFLOAT counter 2.4
"7.4"
```

The preceding commands shown are atomic, which means that they increment/ decrement and return the new value as a single operation. It is not possible for two different clients to execute the same command at the same time and get the same result—no race conditions happen with those commands.

For example, if the *counter* key is *1* and two different clients (A and B) increment their counters at the same time with **INCR**, client A will receive the value *2* and client B will receive *3*.

> Redis is single threaded, which means that it always executes one command at a time. Sometimes, commands are mentioned as atomic, which means that a race condition will never happen when multiple clients try to perform operations on the same key at the same time.

Building a voting system with Strings using Node.js

This section builds a set of Node.js functions used to upvote and downvote articles. The idea is that there is a set of articles, and users can define their popularity by voting up or down.

Now let's save a small collection of articles in Redis using **redis-cli**. We will only add three article headlines to make the example easier to understand. In a real-world situation, you would use a Redis client for your programming language (rather than **redis-cli**), and the articles would be retrieved from a database:

```
$ redis-cli
127.0.0.1:6379> SET article:12345:headline "Google Wants to Turn Your Clothes
Into a Computer"
OK
127.0.0.1:6379> SET article:10001:headline "For Millennials, the End of the TV
Viewing Party"
OK
127.0.0.1:6379> SET article:60056:headline "Alicia Vikander, Who Portrayed
Denmark's Queen, Is Screen Royalty"
OK
```

To complete this example, we will need two keys in Redis for each article. We have already defined our first key to store the headline of each article. Observe this key name structure: *article:<id>:headline*. The second key name will have a similar structure: *article:<id>:votes*. This nomenclature is important in order to create abstractions. The IDs may be passed around, and even if the key format changes, the application logic will remain the same. Also, it is easy to extend the application if other metadata (URL, summary, and so on) needs to be stored.

Our code will have three functions: the first increments the number of votes in an article by *1*, the second decrements the number of votes in an article by *1*, and the third displays the article headline and the number of votes. All three functions (*upVote*, *downVote*, and *showResults*) require the article ID as the argument. Perform the following set of steps:

Create a file called *articles-popularity.js* in the *chapter 1* folder where all of the code from this section should be saved:

```
var redis = require("redis"); // 1
var client = redis.createClient(); // 2

function upVote(id) {  // 3
  var key = "article:" + id + ":votes"; // 4
  client.incr(key);  // 5
}
```

1. Require the *redis* library in Node.js. This is equivalent to *import* in other languages.

2. Create a Redis client instance.

3. Create an *upVote* function that has the article ID as the argument.

4. Define your key name using the *article:<id>:votes* structure.

5. Use the **INCR** command to increment the number of votes by 1.

The function *downVote* is basically the same as *upVote*. The only difference is that it uses the command **DECR** instead of **INCR**:

```
function downVote(id) { // 1
  var key = "article:" + id + ":votes"; // 2
  client.decr(key); // 3
}
```

1. Create a function *downVote* that has the article ID as the argument.

2. Define your key name using the structure *article:<id>:votes* (just as we did in the *upVote* function).

3. Use the **DECR** command to decrement the number of votes by 1.

The function *showResults* shows the article headline and the number of votes that an article has:

```
function showResults(id) {
  var headlineKey = "article:" + id + ":headline";
  var voteKey = "article:" + id + ":votes";
  client.mget([headlineKey, voteKey], function(err, replies) { // 1
    console.log('The article "' + replies[0] + '" has', replies[1],
      'votes'); // 2
  });
}
```

1. Use the **MGET** command to pass an array of keys and a callback function. For every key that does not hold a String value or does not exist, the value *null* is returned.

   In the anonymous function, the argument *replies* has two values: index 0, which has the headline, and index 1, which has the number of votes.

2. Display a message with the article headline and number of votes.

Note:

The Node.js client that we are using is strictly asynchronous. All Redis commands have an optional callback function for handling errors and replies from the Redis server.

In the previous **MGET** example, the only way to handle the key values is by passing a callback to *client.mget()*.

Please make sure you fully understand the idea of callbacks mentioned before. This is necessary in order to understand other examples using Node.js.

It is time to call our functions *upVote*, *downVote*, and *showResults*. Add the following to *articles-popularity.js* too:

```
upVote(12345); // article:12345 has 1 vote
upVote(12345); // article:12345 has 2 votes
upVote(12345); // article:12345 has 3 votes
upVote(10001); // article:10001 has 1 vote
upVote(10001); // article:10001 has 2 votes
downVote(10001); // article:10001 has 1 vote
upVote(60056); // article:60056 has 1 vote

showResults(12345);
showResults(10001);
showResults(60056);

client.quit();
```

Then execute it using the following command line:

```
$ node articles-popularity.js
The article "Google Wants to Turn Your Clothes Into a Computer" has 3
votes
The article "For Millennials, the End of the TV Viewing Party" has 1
votes
The article "Alicia Vikander, Who Portrayed Denmark's Queen, Is Screen
Royalty" has 1 votes
```

Downloading the example code

You can download the example code files from your account at http://www.packtpub.com for all the Packt Publishing books you have purchased. If you purchased this book elsewhere, you can visit http://www.packtpub.com/support and register to have the files e-mailed directly to you.

Lists

Lists are a very flexible data type in Redis because they can act like a simple collection, stack, or queue. Many event systems use Redis's Lists as their queue because Lists' operations ensure that concurrent systems will not overlap popping items from a queue — List commands are atomic. There are blocking commands in Redis's Lists, which means that when a client executes a blocking command in an empty List, the client will wait for a new item to be added to the List. Redis's Lists are linked lists, therefore insertions and deletions from the beginning or the end of a List run in *O(1)*, constant time.

The task of accessing an element in a List runs in *O(N)*, linear time, but accessing the first or last element always runs in constant time.

A List can be encoded and memory optimized if it has less elements than the **list-max-ziplist-entries** configuration and if each element is smaller than the configuration **list-max-ziplist-value** (in bytes). *Chapter 4, Commands (Where the Wild Things Are)* provides more details on these configurations.

The maximum number of elements a List can hold is $2^{32}-1$, which means there can be more than 4 billion elements per List.

Some real-world use cases of Lists are as follows:

- **Event queue**: Lists are used in many tools, including Resque, Celery, and Logstash
- **Storing most recent user posts**: Twitter does this by storing the latest tweets of a user in a List

In this section, we will show you some List commands using the **redis-cli**, and then present a generic task queue system in Node.js.

List examples with redis-cli

Since Lists in Redis are linked lists, there are commands used to insert data into the head and tail of a List. The command **LPUSH** inserts data at the beginning of a List (left push), and the command **RPUSH** inserts data at the end of a List (right push):

```
$ redis-cli
127.0.0.1:6379> LPUSH books "Clean Code"
(integer) 1
127.0.0.1:6379> RPUSH books "Code Complete"
(integer) 2
127.0.0.1:6379> LPUSH books "Peopleware"
(integer) 3
```

The command **LLEN** returns the length of a List. The command **LINDEX** returns the element in a given index (indices are zero-based). Elements in a List are always accessed from left to right, which means that index 0 is the first element, index 1 is the second element, and so on. It is possible to use negative indices to access the tail of the List, in which *-1* is the last element, -2 is penultimate element, and so on. **LINDEX** does not modify a List:

```
$ redis-cli
127.0.0.1:6379> LLEN books
(integer) 3
127.0.0.1:6379> LINDEX books 1
"Clean Code"
```

The command **LRANGE** returns an array with all elements from a given index range, including the elements in both the start and end indices. As we mentioned previously, indices are zero-based and can be positive or negative. See the following example:

```
$ redis-cli
127.0.0.1:6379> LRANGE books 0 1
1) "Peopleware"
2) "Clean Code"
127.0.0.1:6379> LRANGE books 0 -1
1) "Peopleware"
2) "Clean Code"
3) "Code Complete"
```

The command **LPOP** removes and returns the first element of a List. The command **RPOP** removes and returns the last element of a List. Unlike **LINDEX**, both **LPOP** and **RPOP** modify the List:

```
$ redis-cli
127.0.0.1:6379> LPOP books
"Peopleware"
127.0.0.1:6379> RPOP books
"Code Complete"
127.0.0.1:6379> LRANGE books 0 -1
1) "Clean Code"
```

Implementing a generic Queue System

The following implementation is going to use JavaScript prototypes, and it is going to be similar to a class-based solution seen in many programming languages.

Create a file called *queue.js* in the *chapter 1* folder with the following code:

```
function Queue(queueName, redisClient) { // 1
    this.queueName = queueName;  // 2
    this.redisClient = redisClient; // 3
    this.queueKey = 'queues:' + queueName; // 4
    // zero means no timeout
    this.timeout = 0; // 5
}
```

1. Create a function called *Queue*, which receives a queue name and the Redis client object as parameters.

2. Save *queueName* as a property.

3. Save *redisClient* as a property.

4. Set the property *queueKey* to the proper Redis key name, based on the function parameter.

5. Set the property *timeout* to zero, which means that when List commands are executed, they will have no timeout.

We need to implement three methods to perform queue operations: *size*, *push*, and *pop*.

The first method we are going to create is *size*:

```
Queue.prototype.size = function(callback) { // 1
    this.redisClient.llen(this.queueKey, callback); // 2
};
```

1. Create the *Queue* method *size*, which expects a callback as an argument.

2. Execute **LLEN** on the queue key name and pass the callback as an argument. This is necessary because the Redis client is asynchronous.

The implementation of the *push* method is as follows:

```
Queue.prototype.push = function(data) { // 1
    this.redisClient.lpush(this.queueKey, data); // 2
};
```

1. Create the *Queue* method *push* that expects one argument. This argument can be anything that can be represented as a string.

2. Execute **LPUSH** by passing the queue key name and the *data* argument.

As this is a generic queue system and Redis lists only store bytes, we assume that all of the data that is sent to the queue can be transformed into a JavaScript string. If you want to make it more generic, you can use JSON serialization and store the serialized string. The previous example used **LPUSH** because we were implementing a queue, and by definition, items are inserted at the front of the queue and removed from the end of the queue. A helpful way to remember this is FIFO (First In, First Out)—we went from left to right.

The implementation of the *pop* method is as follows:

```
Queue.prototype.pop = function(callback) { // 1
    this.redisClient.brpop(this.queueKey, this.timeout, callback); // 2
};
```

1. Create the *Queue* method *pop*, which expects a callback as an argument.
2. Execute **BRPOP**, passing the queue key name, the queue timeout property, and the callback as arguments.

As we mentioned earlier, elements are inserted at the front of the queue and removed from the end of the queue, which is why **BRPOP** was used (if **RPUSH** was used, then **BLPOP** would be necessary).

The command **BRPOP** removes the last element of a Redis List. If the List is empty, it waits until there is something to remove. **BRPOP** is a blocking version of **RPOP**. However, **RPOP** is not ideal. If the List is empty, we would need to implement some kind of polling by ourselves to make sure that items are handled as soon as they are added to the queue. It is better to take advantage of **BRPOP** and not worry about empty lists.

A concrete producer/consumer implementation is shown next. Different log messages are pushed into the "logs" queue by the producer and then popped by the consumer in another terminal window.

The complete *Queue* code, saved as *queue.js*, is as follows:

```
function Queue(queueName, redisClient) {
    this.queueName = queueName;
    this.redisClient = redisClient;
    this.queueKey = 'queues:' + queueName;
    // zero means no timeout
    this.timeout = 0;
}

Queue.prototype.size = function(callback) {
    this.redisClient.llen(this.queueKey, callback);
};
```

```
Queue.prototype.push = function(data) {
  this.redisClient.lpush(this.queueKey, data);
};

Queue.prototype.pop = function(callback) {
  this.redisClient.brpop(this.queueKey, this.timeout, callback);
};

exports.Queue = Queue; // 1
```

1. This is required to expose *Queue* to different modules. This explicit *export* is specific to Node.js, and it is necessary in order to run *require("./queue")*.

Create a file called *producer-worker.js* in the *chapter 1* folder, which is going to add log events to a queue named "logs", and save the following:

```
var redis = require("redis");
var client = redis.createClient();
var queue = require("./queue"); // 1
var logsQueue = new queue.Queue("logs", client); // 2
var MAX = 5;
for (var i = 0 ; i < MAX ; i++) { // 3
    logsQueue.push("Hello world #" + i); // 4
}
console.log("Created " + MAX + " logs"); // 5
client.quit();
```

1. Require the module *queue*, which we've already created and saved as *queue.js*.
2. Create an instance of the function *Queue* defined in the *queue.js* file.
3. Create a loop that runs five times.
4. Push some logs into the logs queue.
5. Print the number of logs created.

Execute the producer file to push logs into the queue:

```
$ node producer-worker.js
Created 5 logs
```

Save the following code in a file called *consumer-worker.js*:

```
var redis = require("redis");
var client = redis.createClient();
var queue = require("./queue"); // 1
var logsQueue = new queue.Queue("logs", client); // 2
```

```
function logMessages() { // 3
  logsQueue.pop(function(err, replies) { // 4
    var queueName = replies[0];
    var message = replies[1];
    console.log("[consumer] Got log: " + message); // 5

    logsQueue.size(function(err, size) { // 6
      console.log(size + " logs left");
    });

    logMessages(); // 7
  });
}

logMessages(); // 8
```

1. Require the queue module (this is the *queue.js* file).
2. Create a *Queue* instance named *logs* and pass the Redis client to it.
3. Create the function *logMessages*.
4. Retrieve an element from the queue instance using the *pop* method. If the List is empty, this function waits until a new element is added. The timeout is zero and it uses a blocking command, **BRPOP**, internally.
5. Display a message retrieved from the queue.
6. Display the queue size after popping a message from the queue.
7. Call the function (recursively) to repeat the process over and over again. This function runs forever.
8. Call *logMessages* to initialize the queue consumption.

This queue system is completed. Now run the file *consumer-worker.js* and watch the elements being popped in the same order in which they were added by *producer-worker.js*:

```
$ node consumer-worker.js
[consumer] Got log: Hello world #0
4 logs left
[consumer] Got log: Hello world #1
3 logs left
[consumer] Got log: Hello world #2
2 logs left
[consumer] Got log: Hello world #3
1 logs left
[consumer] Got log: Hello world #4
0 logs left
```

This file will run indefinitely. More messages can be added to the queue by executing *producer-worker.js* again in a different terminal, and the consumer will continue reading from the queue as soon as new items are added.

The example shown in this section is not reliable enough to deploy to production. If anything goes wrong with the callbacks that pop from the queue, items may be popped but not properly handled. There is no such thing as a retry or any way to track failures.

A good way of solving the reliability problem is to use an additional queue. Each element that is popped from the queue goes to this additional queue. You must remove the item from this extra queue only if everything has worked correctly. You can monitor this extra queue for stuck elements in order to retry them or create failure alerts. The command **RPOPLPUSH** is very suitable for this situation, because it does a **RPOP** in a queue, then does a **LPUSH** in a different queue, and finally returns the element, all in a single step—it is an atomic command.

Hashes

Hashes are a great data structure for storing objects because you can map fields to values. They are optimized to use memory efficiently and look for data very fast. In a Hash, both the field name and the value are Strings. Therefore, a Hash is a mapping of a String to a String.

Previously, in the String example, we used two separate keys to represent an article headline and its votes (*article:<id>:headline* and *article:<id>:votes*). It is more semantic to use a Hash in that case because the two fields belong to the same object (that is, the article).

Another big advantage of Hashes is that they are memory-optimized. The optimization is based on the **hash-max-ziplist-entries** and **hash-max-ziplist-value** configurations. *Chapter 4, Commands (Where the Wild Things Are)*, provides more details on these configurations.

Internally, a Hash can be a ziplist or a hash table. A ziplist is a dually linked list designed to be memory efficient. In a ziplist, integers are stored as real integers rather than a sequence of characters. Although a ziplist has memory optimizations, lookups are not performed in constant time. On the other hand, a hash table has constant-time lookup but is not memory-optimized.

Instagram had to back-reference 300 million media IDs to user IDs, and they decided to benchmark a Redis prototype using Strings and Hashes. The String solution used one key per media ID and around 21 GB of memory. The Hash solution used around 5 GB with some configuration tweaks. The details can be found at http://instagram-engineering.tumblr.com/post/12202313862/storing-hundreds-of-millions-of-simple-key-value.

This section is going to show the most used Hash commands using **redis-cli**, and then present an application that stores movie metadata in Node.js (similar to the http://www.imdb.com website).

Using Hashes with redis-cli

The command **HSET** sets a value to a field of a given key. The syntax is **HSET** *key* field value.

The command **HMSET** sets multiple field values to a key, separated by spaces. Both **HSET** and **HMSET** create a field if it does not exist, or overwrite its value if it already exists.

The command **HINCRBY** increments a field by a given integer. Both **HINCRBY** and **HINCRBYFLOAT** are similar to **INCRBY** and **INCRBYFLOAT** (not presented in the following code):

```
$ redis-cli
127.0.0.1:6379> HSET movie "title" "The Godfather"
(integer) 1
127.0.0.1:6379> HMSET movie "year" 1972 "rating" 9.2 "watchers" 10000000
OK
127.0.0.1:6379> HINCRBY movie "watchers" 3
(integer) 10000003
```

The command **HGET** retrieves a field from a Hash. The command **HMGET** retrieves multiple fields at once:

```
127.0.0.1:6379> HGET movie "title"
"The Godfather"
127.0.0.1:6379> HMGET movie "title" "watchers"
1) "The Godfather"
2) "10000003"
```

The command **HDEL** deletes a field from a Hash:

```
127.0.0.1:6379> HDEL movie "watchers"
(integer) 1
```

The command **HGETALL** returns an array of all field/value pairs in a Hash:

```
127.0.0.1:6379> HGETALL movie
1) "title"
2) "The Godfather"
3) "year"
4) "1972"
5) "rating"
6) "9.2"
127.0.0.1:6379>
```

It is possible to retrieve only the field names or field values of a Hash with the commands **HKEYS** and **HVALS** respectively.

In the next section, we are going to use Hashes to implement a voting system similar to the one presented with Strings.

A voting system with Hashes and Node.js

This section creates a set of functions to save a link and then upvote and downvote it. This is a very simplified version of something that a website like http://www.reddit.com does.

Create a file called *hash-voting-system.js* in the *chapter 1* folder, where all of the code from this section should be saved:

```
var redis = require("redis"); // 1
var client = redis.createClient(); // 2

function saveLink(id, author, title, link) { // 3
  client.hmset("link:" + id, "author", author, "title", title, "link",
link, "score", 0); // 4
}
```

1. Require the module *redis*.
2. Create a Redis client instance.
3. Create a function *saveLink* that has *id*, *author*, *title*, and *link* as arguments.
4. Use **HMSET** to create a Hash with all fields.

The *upVote* and *downVote* functions use the same command (**HINCRBY**). The only difference is that *downVote* passes a negative number:

```
function upVote(id) { // 1
  client.hincrby("link:" + id, "score", 1); // 2
}
```

```
function downVote(id) { // 3
  client.hincrby("link:" + id, "score", -1); // 4
}
```

1. Create an *upVote* function, which has the link ID as the argument.

2. Use the command **HINCRBY** to increment the field score value.

3. Create a *downVote* function, which has its link ID as the argument.

4. Use the **HINCRBY** command to decrement the field score value. There is no **HDECRBY** command in Hash. The only way to decrement a Hash field is by using **HINCRBY** and a negative number.

The function *showDetails* shows all the fields in a Hash, based on the link ID:

```
function showDetails(id) { // 1
  client.hgetall("link:" + id, function(err, replies) { // 2
    console.log("Title:", replies['title']); // 3
    console.log("Author:", replies['author']); // 3
    console.log("Link:", replies['link']); // 3
    console.log("Score:", replies['score']); // 3
    console.log("-------------------------");
  });
}
```

1. Create a function *showDetails* that has link ID as the argument.

2. Use the **HGETALL** command to retrieve all the fields of a Hash.

3. Display all the fields: *title*, *author*, *link*, and *score*.

Use the previously defined functions to save two links, upvote and downvote them, and then display their details:

```
saveLink(123, "dayvson", "Maxwell Dayvson's Github page", "https://
github.com/dayvson");
upVote(123);
upVote(123);
saveLink(456, "hltbra", "Hugo Tavares's Github page", "https://github.
com/hltbra");
upVote(456);
upVote(456);
downVote(456);
```

```
    showDetails(123);
    showDetails(456);

    client.quit();
```

Then execute *hash-voting-system.js*:

```
$ node hash-voting-system.js
Title: Maxwell Dayvson's Github page
Author: dayvson
Link: https://github.com/dayvson
Score: 2
-------------------------
Title: Hugo Tavares's Github page
Author: hltbra
Link: https://github.com/hltbra
Score: 1
-------------------------
```

The command **HGETALL** may be a problem if a Hash has many fields and uses a lot of memory. It may slow down Redis because it needs to transfer all of that data through the network. A good alternative in such a scenario is the command **HSCAN**.

HSCAN does not return all the fields at once. It returns a cursor and the Hash fields with their values in chunks. **HSCAN** needs to be executed until the returned cursor is 0 in order to retrieve all the fields in a Hash:

```
$ redis-cli
127.0.0.1:6379> HMSET example "field1" "value1"
"field2" "value2" "field3" "value3"
OK
127.0.0.1:6379> HSCAN example 0
1) "0"
2) 1) "field2"
   2) "value2"
   3) "field1"
   4) "value1"
   5) "field3"
   6) "value3"
```

Summary

This chapter began with information about Redis's history and some of its design decisions. We explained how to install Redis and demonstrated that the **redis-cli** tool can be a very powerful tool for debugging and learning Redis.

Some examples in this book that require a programming language are implemented in Node.js. Therefore, a quick reference to JavaScript's syntax and Node.js installation were shown.

Redis data types is an extensive subject, and it has been split into two chapters. This chapter explained how Strings, Lists, and Hashes work. The next chapter will cover Sets, Sorted Sets, Bitmaps, and HyperLogLogs and give practical examples.

2

Advanced Data Types (Earning a Black Belt)

This chapter introduces the Set, Sorted Set, Bitmap, and HyperLogLog data types. It is a continuation from the previous chapter, and it also introduces new commands through **redis-cli** and Node.js, along with some details of the internals of each data type.

Sets

A Set in Redis is an unordered collection of distinct Strings—it's not possible to add repeated elements to a Set. Internally, a Set is implemented as a hash table, which is the reason that some operations are optimized: member addition, removal, and lookup run in *O(1)*, constant time.

The Set memory footprint will be reduced if all the members are integers, and the total number of elements can be as high as the value of the **set-max-intset-entries** configuration. *Chapter 4, Commands (Where the Wild Things Are)*, provides more details about this configuration.

The maximum number of elements that a Set can hold is 2^{32}-1, which means that there can be more than 4 billion elements per Set.

Some use cases for Sets are:

- **Data filtering**: For example, filtering all flights that depart from a given city and arrive in another
- **Data grouping**: Grouping all users who viewed similar products (for example, recommendations on Amazon.com)
- **Membership checking**: Checking whether a user is on a blacklist

Recommended reading:

Read *Redis Set Intersection - Using Sets to Filter Data* at `http://robots.thoughtbot.com/redis-set-intersection-using-sets-to-filter-data`.

Set examples with redis-cli

In this section, we are going to use the **redis-cli** command to explain the most useful Set commands. All examples are based on a music application in which each user has a Set of favorite artists.

In these examples, we will add and remove some favorite artists from a user's account, find the favorite artists that two users have in common, and discover artists based on another user's preferences.

The command **SADD** is responsible for adding one or many members to a Set. **SADD** ignores members that already exist in a Set and returns the number of added members:

```
$ redis-cli
127.0.0.1:6379> SADD user:max:favorite_artists "Arcade Fire" "Arctic Monkeys"
"Belle & Sebastian" "Lenine"
(integer) 4
127.0.0.1:6379> SADD user:hugo:favorite_artists "Daft Punk" "The Kooks" "Arctic
Monkeys"
(integer) 3
```

The command **SINTER** expects one or many Sets and returns an array with the members that belong to every Set. In this example, **SINTER** returns only the favorite artists that both Max and Hugo have on their lists:

```
127.0.0.1:6379> SINTER user:max:favorite_artists user:hugo:favorite_artists
1) "Arctic Monkeys"
```

The command **SDIFF** expects one or many Sets. It returns an array with all members of the first Set that do not exist in the Sets that follow it. In this command, the key name order matters. Any key that does not exist is considered to be an empty Set.

There are two ways of using the command **SDIFF**.

The first example returns the names of artists from *user:max:favorite_artists* that are not present in *user:hugo:favorite_artists*:

```
127.0.0.1:6379> SDIFF user:max:favorite_artists user:hugo:favorite_artists
```

1) "Belle & Sebastian"

2) "Arcade Fire"

3) "Lenine"

The second example returns the names of artists from *user:hugo:favorite_artists* that are not present in *user:max:favorite_artists*:

127.0.0.1:6379> **SDIFF** *user:hugo:favorite_artists user:max:favorite_artists*

1) "Daft Punk"

2) "The Kooks"

The **SUNION** command expects one or many Sets. It returns an array with all members of all Sets. The result has no repeated members.

In this example, **SUNION** returns the names of all artists in both users' Sets of favorite artists:

127.0.0.1:6379> **SUNION** *user:max:favorite_artists user:hugo:favorite_artists*

1) "Lenine"

2) "Daft Punk"

3) "Belle & Sebastian"

4) "Arctic Monkeys"

5) "Arcade Fire"

6) "The Kooks"

The command **SRANDMEMBER** returns random members from a Set. Because Sets are unordered, it is not possible to retrieve elements from a given position:

127.0.0.1:6379> **SRANDMEMBER** *user:max:favorite_artists*

"Arcade Fire"

127.0.0.1:6379> **SRANDMEMBER** *user:max:favorite_artists*

"Lenine"

The command **SISMEMBER** checks whether a member exists in a Set. It returns *1* if the member exists and *0* if it does not.

The command **SREM** removes and returns members from a Set. The command **SCARD** returns the number of members in a Set (also known as cardinality):

127.0.0.1:6379> **SISMEMBER** *user:max:favorite_artists* "Arctic Monkeys"

(integer) 1

127.0.0.1:6379> **SREM** *user:max:favorite_artists* "Arctic Monkeys"

(integer) 1

```
127.0.0.1:6379> SISMEMBER user:max:favorite_artists "Arctic Monkeys"
(integer) 0
127.0.0.1:6379> SCARD user:max:favorite_artists
(integer) 3
```

The command **SMEMBERS** returns an array with all members of a Set:

```
127.0.0.1:6379> SMEMBERS user:max:favorite_artists
1) "Belle & Sebastian"
2) "Arcade Fire"
3) "Lenine"
```

Building a deal tracking system

Yipit, Groupon, and LivingSocial are examples of websites that send daily e-mails to users. These e-mails contain a Set of deals (coupons and discounts) that users are interested in. The deals are based on the area in which they live, as well their preferences.

This section will show how to create functions to mimic the features of these websites:

- Mark a deal as sent to a user
- Check whether a user received a group of deals
- Gather metrics from the sent deals

Every deal is a Redis Set containing all user IDs that have received that deal. In the following examples, deals and users are referenced by IDs. Deal IDs are shown as *deal:123*, and user IDs are shown as *user:123*.

Create a file named *deal-metrics.js* in the *chapter 2* folder, where all of the code from this section should be saved.

The function *markDealAsSent* adds a user to a deal Set. The deal needs to be marked as sent; otherwise, there is no way to check whether it was already sent:

```
var redis = require("redis");
var client = redis.createClient();

function markDealAsSent(dealId, userId) { // 1
  client.sadd(dealId, userId); // 2
}
```

1. Define the function *markDealAsSent*, which expects a deal ID and a user ID as arguments.

2. Execute the command **SADD** to add a user ID to a deal Set.

The *sendDealIfNotSent* function checks whether a user ID belongs to a deal Set. This function sends a deal to a user only if it was not already sent:

```
function sendDealIfNotSent(dealId, userId) { // 1
  client.sismember(dealId, userId, function(err, reply) { // 2
    if (reply) {
      console.log("Deal", dealId, "was already sent to
        user", userId); // 3
    } else {
      console.log("Sending", dealId, "to user", userId); // 4
      // code to send the deal to the user would go here… // 5
      markDealAsSent(dealId, userId); // 6
    }
  });
}
```

1. Define the *sendDealIfNotSent* function, which expects a deal ID and a user ID as arguments.

2. Execute the **SISMEMBER** command to check whether a user ID exists in the deal Set. If **SISMEMBER** returns 1 (which means that the user exists in the deal Set), a message saying that deal was already sent to the user is displayed.

3. If the deal was not sent, we display a message saying that deal was not sent to the user.

4. Optionally, add some code to send an e-mail to the user.

5. Call the *markDealAsSent* function after sending the e-mail.

The function *showUsersThatReceivedAllDeals* displays all user IDs that exist in *all* the deal Sets specified. This could be useful for partnership metrics; for instance, a commercial partner might want a list of all users who received *all* of its deals in a given week:

```
function showUsersThatReceivedAllDeals(dealIds) { // 1
  client.sinter(dealIds, function(err, reply) { // 2
    console.log(reply + " received all of the deals: " + dealIds); // 3
  });
}
```

1. Define the function *showUsersThatReceivedAllDeals*, which receives an array of deal IDs.

2. Execute the command **SINTER** to find all users who received all the specified deals.

3. Display the list of all users who received the specified list of deals.

The function *showUsersThatReceivedAtLeastOneOfTheDeals* displays all user IDs that exist in *any* of the deal Sets specified. This could also be useful for partnership metrics; for example, a partner would be interested in all users who received *any* of its deals in a given week:

```
function showUsersThatReceivedAtLeastOneOfTheDeals(dealIds) { // 1
  client.sunion(dealIds, function(err, reply) { // 2
    console.log(reply + " received at least one of the deals: " +
      dealIds); // 3
  });
}
```

1. Define the function *showUsersThatReceivedAtLeastOneOfTheDeals*, which requires an array of deal IDs.

2. Execute the command **SUNION** to find all users who received at least one of the specified deals.

3. Display the list of users who received at least one of the specified deals.

The following code snippet is an example of how to use the functions defined previously. Add the following code to *deal-metrics.js* too:

```
markDealAsSent('deal:1', 'user:1');
markDealAsSent('deal:1', 'user:2');
markDealAsSent('deal:2', 'user:1');
markDealAsSent('deal:2', 'user:3');

sendDealIfNotSent('deal:1', 'user:1');
sendDealIfNotSent('deal:1', 'user:2');
sendDealIfNotSent('deal:1', 'user:3');

showUsersThatReceivedAllDeals(["deal:1", "deal:2"]);
showUsersThatReceivedAtLeastOneOfTheDeals(["deal:1", "deal:2"]);

client.quit();
```

Then execute the file and check the output, as follows:

```
$ node deal-metrics.js
Deal deal:1 was already sent to user user:1
Deal deal:1 was already sent to user user:2
Sending deal:1 to user user:3
user:1 received all of the deals: deal:1,deal:2
user:2,user:3,user:1 received at least one of the deals: deal:1,deal:2
```

Sorted Sets

A Sorted Set is very similar to a Set, but each element of a Sorted Set has an associated score. In other words, a Sorted Set is a collection of nonrepeating Strings sorted by score. It is possible to have elements with repeated scores. In this case, the repeated elements are ordered lexicographically (in alphabetical order).

Sorted Set operations are fast, but not as fast as Set operations, because the scores need to be compared. Adding, removing, and updating an item in a Sorted Set runs in logarithmic time, $O(log(N))$, where N is the number of elements in a Sorted Set. Internally, Sorted Sets are implemented as two separate data structures:

- A skip list with a hash table. A skip list is a data structure that allows fast search within an ordered sequence of elements.
- A ziplist, based on the **zset-max-ziplist-entries** and **zset-max-ziplist-value** configurations.

 Chapter 4, Commands (Where the Wild Things Are), provides more details about these configurations.

Sorted Sets could be used to:

- Build a real time waiting list for customer service
- Show a leaderboard of a massive online game that displays the top players, users with similar scores, or the scores of your friends
- Build an autocomplete system using millions of words

Sorted Set examples with redis-cli

In this section, we are going to use **redis-cli** to explain some commands to work with Sorted Sets. There are many other commands available for Sorted Sets, but the commands presented here will help you understand those other commands.

The **ZADD** command adds one or many members to a Sorted Set. **ZADD** ignores members that already exist in a Sorted Set. It returns the number of added members:

```
$ redis-cli
127.0.0.1:6379> ZADD leaders 100 "Alice"
(integer) 1
127.0.0.1:6379> ZADD leaders 100 "Zed"
(integer) 1
127.0.0.1:6379> ZADD leaders 102 "Hugo"
(integer) 1
127.0.0.1:6379> ZADD leaders 101 "Max"
(integer) 1
```

Elements are added to a Sorted Set with a score and a String value. There are two ordering criteria: the element score and the element value. If a tie exists between the element scores, the lexicographical order of the element values is used to break the tie. In the preceding example, Alice and Zed have the same score. Therefore, the lexicographical order is used to break the tie; Alice is ranked lower than Zed.

There is a family of commands that can fetch ranges in a Sorted Set: **ZRANGE, ZRANGEBYLEX, ZRANGEBYSCORE, ZREVRANGE, ZREVRANGEBYLEX,** and **ZREVRANGEBYSCORE**. But only **ZRANGE** and **ZREVRANGE** are presented here. These two commands are almost the same. The only difference is in how their results are sorted:

- **ZRANGE** returns elements from the lowest to the highest score, and it uses ascending lexicographical order if a score tie exists
- **ZREVRANGE** returns elements from the highest to the lowest score, and it uses descending lexicographical order if a score tie exists

Both of these commands expect a key name, a start index, and an end index. The indices are zero-based and can be positive or negative values. The following example shows how the **ZREVRANGE** command works:

```
127.0.0.1:6379> ZREVRANGE leaders 0 -1
1) "Hugo"
2) "Max"
3) "Zed"
4) "Alice"
```

Also, it is possible to pass an optional parameter to return the elements with their scores using the keyword **WITHSCORES** (the result is an array with pairs of value and score):

```
127.0.0.1:6379> ZREVRANGE leaders 0 -1 WITHSCORES
1) "Hugo"
2) "102"
3) "Max"
4) "101"
5) "Zed"
6) "100"
7) "Alice"
8) "100"
```

The **ZREM** command removes a member from a Sorted Set:

```
127.0.0.1:6379> ZREM leaders "Hugo"
(integer) 1
127.0.0.1:6379> ZREVRANGE leaders 0 -1
1) "Max"
2) "Zed"
3) "Alice"
```

It is possible to retrieve a score or rank of a specific member in a Sorted Set using the commands **ZSCORE** and **ZRANK/ZREVRANK**:

- **ZSCORE**: This returns the score of a member.
- **ZRANK**: This returns the member rank (or index) ordered from low to high. The member with the lowest score has rank 0.
- **ZREVRANK**: This returns the member rank (or index) ordered from high to low. The member with the highest score has rank 0.

```
127.0.0.1:6379> ZSCORE leaders "Max"
"101"
127.0.0.1:6379> ZRANK leaders "Max"
(integer) 2
127.0.0.1:6379> ZREVRANK leaders "Max"
(integer) 0
```

Building a leaderboard system for an online game

In this section, we are going to build a leaderboard application that can be used in an online game. This application has the following features:

- Add and remove users
- Display the details of a user
- Show the top *x* users
- Show the users who are directly ranked above and below a given user

The solution presented uses JavaScript prototypes as classes. The *LeaderBoard* function acts as a class, and all the features presented are methods. It is possible to create multiple leaderboards with this solution, and it is very easy to extend and add more features.

Create a file named *leaderboard.js* in the *chapter 2* folder, where all of the code from this section should be saved, and add the following block of code to it:

```
var redis = require("redis");
var client = redis.createClient();

function LeaderBoard(key) { // 1
  this.key = key; // 2
}
```

1. Create a function called *LeaderBoard*, which receives a *key* name as a parameter.
2. Save *key* as a property.

The implementation of method *addUser* is as follows:

```
LeaderBoard.prototype.addUser = function(username, score) { // 1
  client.zadd([this.key, score, username], function(err, replies) {// 2
    console.log("User", username,"added to the leaderboard!"); // 3
  });
};
```

1. Create the method *addUser*, which expects *username* and *score* as parameters.
2. Execute the command **ZADD** to insert a member into a Sorted Set.
3. Display a confirmation that a user was added to the leaderboard.

The method *removeUser* is similar to *addUser* but uses **ZREM** instead of **ZADD**:

```
LeaderBoard.prototype.removeUser = function(username) { // 1
  client.zrem(this.key, username, function(err, replies) { // 2
    console.log("User", username, "removed successfully!"); // 3
  });
};
```

1. Create the method *removeUser,* which expects *username* as a parameter.
2. Execute the command **ZREM** to remove a member from a Sorted Set.
3. Display a confirmation that a user was deleted from the leaderboard.

The method *getUserScoreAndRank* displays a user's rank and score by executing the commands **ZSCORE** and **ZREVRANK**:

```
LeaderBoard.prototype.getUserScoreAndRank = function(username) { // 1
  var leaderboardKey = this.key; // 2
  client.zscore(leaderboardKey, username, function(err, zscoreReply) {
// 3
    client.zrevrank(leaderboardKey, username, function(
      err, zrevrankReply) { // 4
      console.log("\nDetails of " + username + ":");
      console.log("Score:", zscoreReply + ", Rank: #" +
        (zrevrankReply + 1)); // 5
    });
  });
};
```

1. Create the method *getUserScoreAndRank,* which expects *username* as a parameter.
2. Create a variable called *leaderboardKey* with the leaderboard key name.
3. Execute the command **ZSCORE** to obtain the score of a given user.
4. Execute the command **ZREVRANK** to obtain the rank of a given user after the command **ZSCORE** is executed.
5. Display the user's score and rank.

The method *showTopUsers* is very straightforward because the command **ZREVRANGE** returns a range of members ordered from highest to lowest score:

```
LeaderBoard.prototype.showTopUsers = function(quantity) { // 1
  client.zrevrange([this.key, 0, quantity - 1, "WITHSCORES"],
function(err,
    reply) { // 2
    console.log("\nTop", quantity, "users:");
```

```
    for (var i = 0, rank = 1 ; i < reply.length ; i += 2, rank++) {// 3
      console.log("#" + rank, "User: " + reply[i] + ", score:",
        reply[i + 1]);
    }
  });
};
```

1. Create the method *showTopUsers*, which expects the quantity of top players.

2. Execute **ZREVRANGE** to obtain the top players defined by the variable *quantity*.

3. Iterate over the array of top players and display their ranks, usernames, and scores. The increment of 2 (*i* += 2) is necessary because the returned array is composed of pairs of username and score.

The method *getUsersAroundUser* is used to get a list of users who are ranked relative to a given user in the leaderboard:

```
LeaderBoard.prototype.getUsersAroundUser = function(username,
quantity, callback) { // 1
  var leaderboardKey = this.key; // 2
  client.zrevrank(leaderboardKey, username, function(err,
zrevrankReply) { // 3

    var startOffset = Math.floor(zrevrankReply - (quantity / 2) + 1);
// 4
    if (startOffset < 0) { // 5
      startOffset = 0;
    }
    var endOffset = startOffset + quantity - 1; // 6

    client.zrevrange([leaderboardKey, startOffset, endOffset,
"WITHSCORES"],
        function(err, zrevrangeReply) { // 7
        var users = []; // 8
        for (var i = 0, rank = 1 ; i < zrevrangeReply.length ; i += 2,
          rank++) { // 9
          var user = {
            rank: startOffset + rank,
            score: zrevrangeReply[i + 1],
            username: zrevrangeReply[i],
          }; // 10
          users.push(user); // 11
        }
        callback(users); // 12
```

```
      });
    });
  };
```

1. Create the method *getUsersAroundUser*, which expects a username, the number of users to return, and a callback to be executed with the details of these users.

2. Save *leaderboardkey* as a local variable.

3. Executed **ZREVRANK** to obtain the user's rank (from highest to lowest).

4. Define the variable *startOffset* to get the index value of the first element of the result.

5. Set the variable *startOffset* to zero if it is a negative value.

6. Define the variable *endOffset* to get the index value of the last element of the result.

7. Execute the command **ZREVRANGE** to retrieve the names of all users (and their scores) who are between *startOffset* and *endOffset*.

8. Create the variable *users* as an empty array.

9. Iterate over all users and their scores.

10. Assign user details to the variable *user*.

11. Add user details to the array *users*.

12. Execute the callback function with the array *users*.

The following code snippet is an example that shows how to use the previously defined functions. Add the following code to *leaderboard.js* too:

```
var leaderBoard = new LeaderBoard("game-score");
leaderBoard.addUser("Arthur", 70);
leaderBoard.addUser("KC", 20);
leaderBoard.addUser("Maxwell", 10);
leaderBoard.addUser("Patrik", 30);
leaderBoard.addUser("Ana", 60);
leaderBoard.addUser("Felipe", 40);
leaderBoard.addUser("Renata", 50);
leaderBoard.addUser("Hugo", 80);
leaderBoard.removeUser("Arthur");

leaderBoard.getUserScoreAndRank("Maxwell");

leaderBoard.showTopUsers(3);
```

```
leaderBoard.getUsersAroundUser("Felipe", 5, function(users) { // 1
  console.log("\nUsers around Felipe:");
  users.forEach(function(user) {
    console.log("#" + user.rank, "User:", user.username + ", score:",
      user.score);
  });
  client.quit(); // 2
});
```

1. Execute the method *getUsersAroundUser*, passing *Felipe* as the username, 5 as the number of users to return, and a callback that displays the details of the users who are ranked relative to *Felipe*.

2. Close the Redis connection after all the commands are executed.

 In all other examples, the method *quit()* was not called inside of any function/method, but in the previous example, it was necessary. This is because there were nested callback functions, and the *quit()* function does not wait for all nested callbacks to be handled.

Then execute the file and check the output:

```
$ node leaderboards.js
User Arthur added to the leaderboard!
User KC added to the leaderboard!
User Maxwell added to the leaderboard!
User Patrik added to the leaderboard!
User Ana added to the leaderboard!
User Felipe added to the leaderboard!
User Renata added to the leaderboard!
User Hugo added to the leaderboard!
User Arthur removed successfully!

Top 3 users:
#1 User: Hugo, score: 80
#2 User: Ana, score: 60
#3 User: Renata, score: 50

Details of Maxwell:
Score: 10, Rank: #7

Users around Felipe:
#2 User: Ana, score: 60
#3 User: Renata, score: 50
```

```
#4 User: Felipe, score: 40
#5 User: Patrik, score: 30
#6 User: KC, score: 20
```

Sorted Sets are one of the richest data types in Redis. We covered the commands that we believe are the most useful, but you can check out the online documentation to learn more.

Bitmaps

A Bitmap is not a real data type in Redis. Under the hood, a Bitmap is a String. We can also say that a Bitmap is a set of bit operations on a String. However, we are going to consider them as data types because Redis provides commands to manipulate Strings as Bitmaps. Bitmaps are also known as bit arrays or bitsets.

A Bitmap is a sequence of bits where each bit can store 0 or 1. You can think of a Bitmap as an array of ones and zeroes. The Redis documentation refers to Bitmap indices as *offsets*. The application domain dictates what each Bitmap index means.

Bitmaps are memory efficient, support fast data lookups, and can store up to 2^{32} bits (more than 4 billion bits).

See this example of a Bitmap with three bits turned on and two turned off:

offset 0	offset 1	offset 2	offset 3	offset 4
1	0	0	1	1

A Bitmap with one Set on offsets 0, 3, and 4 and zero Set on offsets 1 and 2

In order to see how a Bitmap can be memory efficient, we are going to compare a Bitmap to a Set. The comparison scenario is an application that needs to store all user IDs that visited a website on a given day (the Bitmap offset represents a user ID). We assume that our application has 5 million users in total, but only 2 million users visited the website on that day, and that each user ID can be represented by 4 bytes (32 bits, which is the size of an integer in a 32-bit computer).

The following table compares how much memory a Bitmap and a Set implementation would take to store 2 million user IDs. In this example, the Redis key is the date of visits:

Redis key	Data type	Amount of bits per user	Stored users	Total memory
visits:2015-01-01	Bitmap	1 bit	5 million	*1 * 5000000 bits = 625kB*
visits:2015-01-01	Set	32 bits	2 million	*32 * 2000000 bits = 8MB*

The worst-case scenario for the Bitmap implementation is represented in the preceding table. It had to allocate memory for the entire user base even though only 2 million users visited the page. This happens when the user with the highest ID visits the page (user ID *5000000*).

Even when it comes to allocating memory to users that did not visit the page, the Bitmap implementation uses far less memory than the Set implementation.

However, Bitmaps are not always memory efficient. If we change the previous example to consider only 100 visits instead of 2 million, assuming the worst case-scenario again, the Bitmap implementation would not be memory-efficient, as shown here:

Redis key	Data type	Amount of bits per user	Stored users	Total memory
visits:2015-01-01	Bitmap	1 bit	5 million	*1 * 5000000 bits = 625kB*
visits:2015-01-01	Set	32 bits	100	*32 * 100 bits = 3.125kB*

Bitmaps are a great match for applications that involve real-time analytics, because they can tell whether a user performed an action (that is, "Did user X perform action Y today?") or how many times an event occurred (that is, "How many users performed action Y this week?"):

- Did user 1 read *Redis Essentials* today?
- Did user 1 play *Angry Birds* this week?
- How many users read *Redis Essentials* last month?
- How many users played *Angry Birds* this year?

Bitmap examples with redis-cli

The **redis-cli** examples show how to use Bitmap commands to store user IDs of users who visited a web page on a given day. Each user is identified by an ID, which is a sequential integer. Each Bitmap offset represents a user: user 1 is offset 1, user 30 is offset 30, and so on.

The Bitmap approach presented here consists of giving a bit the value of 1 if a user visited a page and 0 if they did not, like this:

user 0	user 1	user 2	user 3	user 4
offset 0	offset 1	offset 2	offset 3	offset 4
1	0	0	1	1

The previous Bitmap is 10011, and it means that users 0, 3, and 4 visited the website — because they are marked as 1 — and the other users did not visit the website.

The **SETBIT** command is used to give a value to a Bitmap offset, and it accepts only 1 or 0. If the Bitmap does not exist, it creates it. In the following snippet, users 10 and 15 visited the website on *2015-01-01*, and users 10 and 11 visited it on *2015-01-02*:

```
127.0.0.1:6379> SETBIT visits:2015-01-01 10 1
(integer) 0
127.0.0.1:6379> SETBIT visits:2015-01-01 15 1
(integer) 0
127.0.0.1:6379> SETBIT visits:2015-01-02 10 1
(integer) 0
127.0.0.1:6379> SETBIT visits:2015-01-02 11 1
(integer) 0
```

The **GETBIT** command returns the value of a Bitmap offset. In the following example, it checks whether user 10 visited the website on 2015-01-01, and then checks whether user 15 visited the website on 2015-01-02:

```
127.0.0.1:6379> GETBIT visits:2015-01-01 10
(integer) 1
127.0.0.1:6379> GETBIT visits:2015-01-02 15
(integer) 0
```

The **BITCOUNT** command returns the number of bits marked as 1 in a Bitmap. In this example, it returns the number of users who visited the website on the specified dates:

```
127.0.0.1:6379> BITCOUNT visits:2015-01-01
(integer) 2
127.0.0.1:6379> BITCOUNT visits:2015-01-02
(integer) 2
```

The **BITOP** command requires a destination key, a bitwise operation, and a list of keys to apply to that operation and store the result in the destination key. The available bitwise operations are *OR*, *AND*, *XOR*, and *NOT*. The following example uses **BITOP OR** to find out how many users visited the website on the specified dates (2015-01-01 and 2015-01-02):

```
127.0.0.1:6379> BITOP OR total_users visits:2015-01-01 visits:2015-01-02
(integer) 2
127.0.0.1:6379> BITCOUNT total_users
(integer) 3
```

Building web analytics

This section creates a simple web analytics system to save and count daily user visits to a website and then retrieve user IDs from the visits on a given date.

Create a file called *metrics-bitmap.js* in the *chapter 2* folder, where all of the code from this section should be saved.

The function *storeDailyVisit* uses the command **SETBIT** to save a given user ID of a user who visited the website on a given date:

```
var redis = require("redis");
var client = redis.createClient({return_buffers: true}); // 1

function storeDailyVisit(date, userId) { // 2
  var key = 'visits:daily:' + date; // 3
  client.setbit(key, userId, 1, function(err, reply) { // 4
    console.log("User", userId, "visited on", date); // 5
  });
}
```

1. Create a Redis client that uses Node.js buffers rather than JavaScript strings — this line is different from the previous examples. It is simpler to manipulate bytes with buffers than with JavaScript strings.

2. Create the function *storeDailyVisit*, which expects a date and a user ID. The date should be in this format: *YYYY-MM-DD* (for example, *2015-01-01*).

3. Create a variable called *key* with the format *visits:daily:YYYY-MM-DD*.

4. Execute the command **SETBIT** on the key that was newly created, using the variable *userId* for the offset and *1* for the bit value. This means that *userId* visited the website on that date.

5. Display a confirmation message.

The function *countVisits* uses the command **BITCOUNT** to count the number of users who visited the website on a given date:

```
function countVisits(date) { // 1
  var key = 'visits:daily:' + date; // 2
  client.bitcount(key, function(err, reply) { // 3
    console.log(date, "had", reply, "visits."); // 4
  });
}
```

1. Create the function *countVisits*, which expects a date in the format *YYYY-MM-DD*.

2. Create a variable called *key* with the format as *visits:daily:YYYY-MM-DD*.

3. Execute the command **BITCOUNT** on the newly created key .

4. Display the number of users who visited the website on a given date.

The function *showUserIdsFromVisit* displays the user IDs of all users who visited the website on a given date. It uses the command **GET** to retrieve the Bitmap and then iterates over each bit to find the IDs of the users who visited the website on the given date. This feature is not easy to implement using **redis-cli**. This is because it requires iterations and bitwise operations on every bit of the Bitmap:

```
function showUserIdsFromVisit(date) { // 1
  var key = 'visits:daily:' + date; // 2
  client.get(key, function(err, bitmapValue) { // 3
    var userIds = []; // 4
    var data = bitmapValue.toJSON().data; // 5

    data.forEach(function(byte, byteIndex) { // 6
      for (var bitIndex = 7 ; bitIndex >= 0 ; bitIndex--) { // 7
        var visited = byte >> bitIndex & 1; // 8
```

```
        if (visited === 1) { // 9
          var userId = byteIndex * 8 + (7 - bitIndex); // 10
          userIds.push(userId); // 11
        }
      }
    });
    console.log("Users " + userIds + " visited on " + date); // 12
  });
}
```

1. Create the function *showUserIdsFromVisit*, which expects a date in the *YYYY-MM-DD* format as the argument.

2. Create a Redis key.

3. Execute the command **GET** to retrieve the Bitmap value. This returns a Node.js Buffer, not a String (because of the *return_buffers* option passed to *redis.createClient*).

4. Create an empty array and assigned it to the variable *userIds*. This variable will store all the user IDs to be displayed.

5. Assign the Bitmap value to the variable *data*.

6. Iterate over the bytes of the Bitmap.

7. Iterate over each bit of a byte. Each byte has 8 bits, and the iteration is from right to left, because this is how Redis stores the data in an x86 machine.

8. Shift a byte to the right to remove the bits that were already worked on. Then we applied a bitmask of 1 and assigned the result to the variable *visited*. In other words, this line checks whether the current bit is 1.

9. Check whether the user visited the page.

10. Recreate the user ID. This multiplies the current byte index by 8, subtracts the current bit index from 7, and then adds the two results.

    For instance, if the byte being worked on is the first, *byteIndex* is *0*. If the bit being worked on is also the first, *bitIndex* is *7*. Therefore, the first bit of the first byte is *user 0 (0 * 8 + (7 - 7) = 0)*. The multiplication by 8 is necessary because each byte stores at most eight users. The subtraction of 7 is to identify the user from the eight different possibilities.

    Another example would be user 10, which is in the second byte. The value of *byteIndex* would be 1, and *bitIndex* would be 5 *(1 * 8 + (7 - 5) = 8 + 2 = 10)*.

11. This last snippet stores some visits, counts them, and then displays the IDs of the users who visited the website on a given date:

```
storeDailyVisit('2015-01-01', '1');
storeDailyVisit('2015-01-01', '2');
storeDailyVisit('2015-01-01', '10');
storeDailyVisit('2015-01-01', '55');

countVisits('2015-01-01');
showUserIdsFromVisit('2015-01-01');

client.quit();
```

Then execute the *metrics-bitmap.js* file:

```
$ node metrics-bitmap.js
User 1 visited on 2015-01-01
User 2 visited on 2015-01-01
User 10 visited on 2015-01-01
User 500000 visited on 2015-01-01
2015-01-01 had 4 visits
Users 1,2,10,500000 visited on 2015-01-01
```

 This example only stores visits once. Subsequent visits by the same user on the same date are not counted. If you want to know the total number of visits, you should use a String as a separate counter. Every time a visit occurs, **INCR** should be executed on that counter.

All the examples shown in this section can be adapted to perform analytics in a variety of contexts: analyzing users watching videos, playing songs, opening e-mails, clicking on links, and so on.

HyperLogLogs

A HyperLogLog is not actually a real data type in Redis. Conceptually, a HyperLogLog is an algorithm that uses randomization in order to provide a very good approximation of the number of unique elements that exist in a Set. It is fascinating because it only runs in $O(1)$, constant time, and uses a very small amount of memory—up to 12 kB of memory per key. Although technically a HyperLogLog is not a real data type, we are going to consider it as one because Redis provides specific commands to manipulate Strings in order to calculate the cardinality of a set using the HyperLogLog algorithm.

The HyperLogLog algorithm is probabilistic, which means that it does not ensure 100 percent accuracy. The Redis implementation of the HyperLogLog has a standard error of 0.81 percent. In theory, there is no practical limit for the cardinality of the sets that can be counted.

The HyperLogLog algorithm was described originally in the paper *HyperLogLog: The analysis of a near-optimal cardinality estimation algorithm* by Philippe Flajolet, Éric Fusy, Olivier Gandouet, and Frédéric Meunier.

HyperLogLogs were introduced in Redis 2.8.9. There are only three commands for HyperLogLogs: **PFADD**, **PFCOUNT**, and **PFMERGE**.

[The prefix PF is in honor of *Philippe Flajolet*, the author of the algorithm. He passed away in March 2011.]

Usually, to perform unique counting, you need an amount of memory proportional to the number of items in the set that you are counting. HyperLogLogs solve these kinds of problems with great performance, low computation cost, and a small amount of memory. However, it is important to remember that HyperLogLogs are not 100 percent accurate. Nonetheless, in some cases, 99.19 percent is good enough.

Here are a few examples of where HyperLogLogs can be used:

- Counting the number of unique users who visited a website
- Counting the number of distinct terms that were searched for on your website on a specific date or time
- Counting the number of distinct hashtags that were used by a user
- Counting the number of distinct words that appear in a book

Counting unique users – HyperLogLog versus Set

This section compares how much memory a HyperLogLog and a Set would need to count the unique visits to a given website per hour.

Let's look at the following scenario: a website has an average of 100,000 unique visits per hour. Each user who visits the page is identified by a UUID (universally unique identifier), which is represented by a 32-byte string (for example, **de305d54-75b4-431b-adb2-eb6b9e546014**).

In order to store all unique visitors, a Redis key is created for every hour of a day. This means that in a day, there are 24 keys, and in a month there are 720 keys (*24 * 30*).

A HyperLogLog uses up to 12 kB to store 100,000 unique visits (or any cardinality). On the other hand, a Set uses 3.2 MB to store 100,000 UUIDs that are 32 bytes each.

The following table shows how much memory each data type would need to store 100,000 unique user visits in an hour, a day, and a month:

Data type	Memory in an hour	Memory in a day	Memory in a month
HyperLogLog	12 kB	*12 kB * 24 = 288 kB*	*288 kB * 30 = 8.4 MB*
Set	*32 bytes * 100000 = 3.2 MB*	*3.2 MB * 24 = 76.8 MB*	*76.8 MB * 30 = 2.25 GB*

For this situation, a HyperLogLog is more suitable than a Set.

HyperLogLogs examples with redis-cli

The **redis-cli** examples show how you can use HyperLogLog commands to record and count unique user visits to a website.

The command **PFADD** adds one or many strings to a HyperLogLog. **PFADD** returns 1 if the cardinality was changed and 0 if it remains the same:

```
$ redis-cli
127.0.0.1:6379> PFADD visits:2015-01-01 "carl" "max" "hugo" "arthur"
(integer) 1
127.0.0.1:6379> PFADD visits:2015-01-01 "max" "hugo"
(integer) 0
127.0.0.1:6379> PFADD visits:2015-01-02 "max" "kc" "hugo" "renata"
(integer) 1
```

The command **PFCOUNT** accepts one or many keys as arguments. When a single argument is specified, it returns the approximate cardinality. When multiple keys are specified, it returns the approximate cardinality of the union of all unique elements:

```
127.0.0.1:6379> PFCOUNT visits:2015-01-01
(integer) 4
127.0.0.1:6379> PFCOUNT visits:2015-01-02
(integer) 4
127.0.0.1:6379> PFCOUNT visits:2015-01-01 visits:2015-01-02
(integer) 6
```

The command **PFMERGE** requires a destination key and one or many HyperLogLog keys as arguments. It merges all the specified HyperLogLogs and stores the result in the destination key:

```
127.0.0.1:6379> PFMERGE visits:total visits:2015-01-01 visits:2015-01-02
OK
127.0.0.1:6379> PFCOUNT visits:total
(integer) 6
```

Counting and retrieving unique website visits

This section extends the previous **redis-cli** example using Node.js and adds an hour as granularity. Later, it merges the 24 keys that represent each hour of a day into a single key. A more feature-complete implementation version of this example will be presented in *Chapter 3, Time Series (A Collection of Observations)*.

Create a file called *unique-visitors.js* in the *chapter 2* folder, where all of the code from this section should be saved.

The function *addVisit* registers a unique visit. Add the following code to *unique-visitors.js*:

```
var redis = require('redis');
var client = redis.createClient();

function addVisit(date, user) { // 1
  var key = 'visits:' + date; // 2
  client.pfadd(key, user); // 3
}
```

1. Create the function *addVisit*, which requires a date and a username. The date can be in *YYYY-MM-DD* or *YYYY-MM-DDTH* format (for example, 2015-01-01 or 2015-01-01T2).

2. Create a variable called *key* in the format we just described.

3. Execute the command **PFADD** to add the user to the HyperLogLog key.

The function *count* displays the number of unique visits on the specified dates:

```
function count(dates) { // 1
  var keys = []; // 2
  dates.forEach(function(date, index) { // 3
```

```
    keys.push('visits:' + date);
  });

  client.pfcount(keys, function(err, reply) { // 4
    console.log('Dates', dates.join(', '), 'had', reply, 'visits');
  });
}
```

1. Create the function *count*, which requires an array of dates.
2. Create the variable *keys* and assigned an empty array to it.
3. Iterate over each date from the *dates* parameter, prepended *visits:* to it, and then appended it to the variable *keys*.
4. Execute the command **PFCOUNT** and displayed the result.

The function *aggregateDate* merges the visits on a given date:

```
function aggregateDate(date) { // 1
  var keys = ['visits:' + date]; // 2
  for (var i = 0; i < 24; i++) { // 3
    keys.push('visits:' + date + 'T' + i); // 4
  }
  client.pfmerge(keys, function(err, reply) { // 5
    console.log('Aggregated date', date);
  });
}
```

1. Create the function *aggregateDate*, which requires a date as a parameter.
2. Create the variable *keys* and assign to it an array with the formatted date (for example, *visits:2015-01-01*).
3. Loop through every hour of a day.
4. Append a formatted date to the variable *keys* (*YYYY-MM-DDTH*).
5. Execute the command **PFMERGE** to merge visits from all 24 hours of a day and store them in the destination key (indicated by the variable *date*).

The following sample simulates 200 users visiting the page 1,000 times in a period of 24 hours. It also counts the number of users who visited the page during the hour *2015-01-01T0*:

```
var MAX_USERS = 200; // 1
var TOTAL_VISITS = 1000; // 2

for (var i = 0; i < TOTAL_VISITS; i++) { // 3
```

```
  var username = 'user_' + Math.floor(1 + Math.random() * MAX_USERS);
// 4
  var hour = Math.floor(Math.random() * 24); // 5
  addVisit('2015-01-01T' + hour, username); // 6
}

count(['2015-01-01T0']); // 7
count(['2015-01-01T5', '2015-01-01T6', '2015-01-01T7']); // 8

aggregateDate('2015-01-01'); // 9
count(['2015-01-01']); // 10

client.quit();
```

1. Define the variable *MAX_USERS* with a value of 200.

2. Define the variable *TOTAL_VISITS* with a value of 1000.

3. Iterate from 0 to *TOTAL_VISITS*.

4. Create a username randomly and assigned it to the variable *username*, based on the variable *MAX_USERS*. The lowest username will be *user_1* and the highest will be *user_200*.

5. Create an hour randomly and assigned it to the variable *hour*. The lowest hour will be *0* and the highest will be *23*.

6. Call the function *addVisit*, passing a formatted date and username (both randomly generated). It is possible for *addVisit* to be called with the same parameters several times. In this scenario, the HyperLogLog's cardinality is not changed, since HyperLogLogs only take unique values into consideration.

After the preceding code is saved in *unique-visitors.js*, execute the file to get the following output:

```
$ node unique-visitors.js
Dates 2015-01-01T0 had 41 visits
Dates 2015-01-01T5, 2015-01-01T6, 2015-01-01T7 had 97 visits
Aggregated date 2015-01-01
Dates 2015-01-01 had 203 visits
```

This simulation uses random data, so it is likely that the output will be slightly different.

Summary

This chapter presented advanced data types: Sets, Sorted Sets, Bitmaps, and HyperLogLogs. These were presented along with real use cases and examples using **redis-cli** and Node.js.

The next chapter is going to explain how to build a feature-complete Time Series system with Redis in Node.js using Strings, Hashes, and HyperLogLogs. It will support querying multiple granularities, data consolidation, and automatic data expiration.

3

Time Series (A Collection of Observations)

A time series is an ordered sequence of values (data points) made over a time interval. Time series are used in statistics, social networks, and communications engineering. Actually, they can be adopted in any domain that needs temporal measurements. They can be used to predict future stock market changes, real estate trends, environmental conditions, and more.

Examples of time series are:

- Usage of specific words or terms in a newspaper over time
- Minimum wage year-by-year
- Daily changes in stock prices
- Product purchases month-by-month
- Climate changes

Many time series systems face challenges with storage, since a dataset can grow too large very quickly. When storing events every second, at least 86,400 data points are created every day, and storing so many data points over a long period of time is challenging, especially for in-memory data stores, such as Redis.

Another aspect of a time series is that as time goes by, the smallest granularities lose their values. For instance, if events are recorded for a full month, usually analysis is done by hours or days, but rarely by seconds. There would be too many data points to be analyzed, so it would not provide much value.

The New York Times created an interesting tool called Chronicle that graphs the use of words and phrases in its newspaper issues since 1851. The following screenshot represents the percentage of articles that contained the word "war." We recommend that you check out the tool at `http://chronicle.nytlabs.com`.

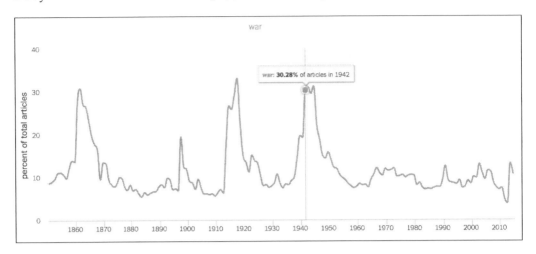

In the previous graph, we can see that the term "war" was present in about 30 percent of the articles in The New York Times in 1942 (during World War II). Thus, it is possible to identify a period of war by reading the graph.

Chronicle only displays results on a yearly basis, which means that it is not possible to see the percentage of words used per month or day. It is a good tool for historical analysis, but it does not provide insights into monthly or daily word trends.

In this chapter, a library in Node.js will be created to exemplify how to implement a time series in Redis using the String, Hash, Sorted Set, and HyperLogLog data types. This library records events per second, minute, hour, and day. It also provides query functions to retrieve the data over time.

Time Series is a very extensive subject and there are a lot of published papers and books about it, so the examples shown here are not going to cover all sorts of problems; they are meant to be simple and easy to understand.

Building the foundation

In this section, we will demonstrate how to create a simple time series library using Redis Strings. This library will be able to save an event that happened at a given timestamp with a method called *insert*. It will also provide a method called *fetch* to fetch values within a range of timestamps.

Later on, we will make this library memory-efficient using Hashes instead of Strings, and also add a feature to store and search for unique events in a given timestamp range using Sorted Sets and HyperLogLogs.

The solution supports multiple granularities: day, hour, minute, and second. Every time an event happens in the system, an increment is stored for that specific time in multiple granularities.

For instance, if an event happens on date 01/01/2015 at 00:00:00 (represented by the timestamp 1420070400), the following Redis keys will be incremented (one key per granularity):

- *events:1sec:1420070400*
- *events:1min:1420070400*
- *events:1hour:1420070400*
- *events:1day:1420070400*

All events are grouped by granularities, which means that an event that happened at 02:04:01 will be saved with an event that happened at 02:04:02 — both happened at the same minute. The same grouping rules apply to the hour and day granularities.

This solution is very good for storing event counts that are near real-time, such as:

- Page views
- Video views
- Number of clicks
- Number of purchased items

Create a file called *timeseries-string.js* in the *chapter 3* folder (where all of the code from this section should be saved):

```
function TimeSeries(client, namespace) { // 1
  this.namespace = namespace; // 2
  this.client = client; // 3
  this.units = { // 4
    second: 1,
    minute: 60,
    hour: 60 * 60,
    day: 24 * 60 * 60
  };

  this.granularities = { // 5
```

```
    '1sec'  : { name: '1sec', ttl: this.units.hour * 2,
                        duration: this.units.second },// 6
    '1min'  : { name: '1min', ttl: this.units.day * 7,
                        duration: this.units.minute },// 7
    '1hour': { name: '1hour', ttl: this.units.day * 60 ,
                        duration: this.units.hour },// 8
    '1day'  : { name: '1day', ttl: null, duration: this.units.day } // 9
  };
};
```

1. Create the function *TimeSeries*, which requires a Redis client and a namespace as the parameters.

2. Save *namespace* as a property.

3. Save *client* as a property, which should be a Redis client object.

4. Create the property *units* with granularity names and their equivalents in seconds (for example, an hour has 3,600 seconds, which means 60 minutes x 60 seconds).

5. Create the property *granularities*, which has the granularity names as keys. Each granularity is an object with a name, a Time to Live (TTL), and a duration. For instance, the granularity *1sec* has a TTL of 2 hours, and its duration is 1 second. The *null* TTL present on *1day* means that this granularity never expires.

The method *insert* registers an event that happened at a given timestamp in multiple granularities:

```
TimeSeries.prototype.insert = function(timestampInSeconds) { // 1
  for (var granularityName in this.granularities) { // 2
    var granularity = this.granularities[granularityName]; // 3
    var key = this._getKeyName(granularity, timestampInSeconds); // 4
    this.client.incr(key); // 5
    if (granularity.ttl !== null) { // 6
      this.client.expire(key, granularity.ttl); // 7
    }
  }
};
```

1. Create the method *insert*, which receives a timestamp as an argument.

2. Iterate over all granularities.

3. Assign the current granularity to the variable *granularity*.

4. Call the private method *_getKeyName*, which returns a key name in the format "namespace:granularity:timestamp" (for example, "pageviews:1sec:1000").

5. Execute the **INCR** command, passing the variable *key*.

6. Verify that the current granularity is not *null*.

7. Execute the command **EXPIRE**, passing the variable key and the current granularity TTL. This command deletes a Redis key automatically after a given number of seconds.

The private method *_getKeyName* returns a key name, based on the granularity and the timestamp:

```
TimeSeries.prototype._getKeyName = function(granularity,
timestampInSeconds) { // 1
  var roundedTimestamp = this._getRoundedTimestamp(timestampInSeconds,
granularity.duration); // 2
  return [this.namespace, granularity.name, roundedTimestamp].
join(':'); // 3
};
```

1. Create the method *_getKeyName*, which receives a granularity object and a timestamp. It is a convention in JavaScript to use an underscore at the beginning of private method names.

2. Execute the method *_getRoundedTimestamp*. It returns a normalized timestamp by granularity duration. This new timestamp will be used to create the key name. For instance, all insertions that happen in the first minute of an hour are stored in a key like "namespace:1min:0", all inserts from the second minute are stored in "namespace:1min:60", and so on.

The private method *_getRoundedTimestamp* returns a normalized timestamp, based on a value. For instance, if the *precision* variable is 60, any timestamp between 0 and 60 will result in 0, any timestamp between 60 and 120 will result in 60, and so on:

```
TimeSeries.prototype._getRoundedTimestamp =
function(timestampInSeconds, precision) { // 1
  return Math.floor(timestampInSeconds/precision) * precision; // 2
};
```

1. Create the method *_getRoundedTimestamp*, which receives a timestamp in seconds and a precision value.

2. Return a normalized timestamp based on the precision.

The method *fetch* executes a callback by passing an array of data points, based on a given granularity and a range of timestamps:

```
TimeSeries.prototype.fetch = function(granularityName, beginTimestamp,
endTimestamp, onComplete) { // 1
  var granularity = this.granularities[granularityName]; // 2
  var begin = this._getRoundedTimestamp(beginTimestamp,  granularity.
duration); // 3
  var end = this._getRoundedTimestamp(endTimestamp, granularity.
duration); // 4
  var keys = []; // 5

  for (var timestamp = begin; timestamp <= end; timestamp +=
granularity.duration) { // 6
    var key = this._getKeyName(granularity, timestamp); // 7
    keys.push(key); // 8
  }

  this.client.mget(keys, function(err, replies) { // 9
    var results = []; // 10
    for (var i = 0 ; i < replies.length ; i++) { // 11
      var timestamp = beginTimestamp + i * granularity.duration; // 12
      var value = parseInt(replies[i], 10) || 0; // 13
      results.push({timestamp: timestamp , value: value}); // 14
    }
    onComplete(granularityName, results); // 15
  });
};

exports.TimeSeries = TimeSeries; // 16
```

1. Create the method *fetch*, which receives a granularity name, a beginning timestamp, an end timestamp, and a callback.

2. Assign the current granularity to the variable *granularity*.

3. Assign the normalized variable *beginTimestamp* to the variable *begin*, based on the current granularity duration.

4. Assign the normalized variable *endTimestamp* to the variable *end*, based on the current granularity duration.

5. Create the variable *keys* and assign an empty array to it.

6. Iterate over all the timestamps in the specified range. Each iteration step is to be incremented by the duration of the granularity.

7. Call the private method *_getKeyName* in order to find the key name of the current timestamp.

8. Add the variable *key* to the variable *keys*.

9. Execute the command **MGET**, passing all timestamp key names as well as a callback.

10. Create the variable *results* and assign an empty array to it.

11. Iterate over all **MGET** replies.

12. Calculate a timestamp for each reply based on the *beginTimestamp* variable.

13. Convert a reply value to an integer value. If this is not possible, fall back to zero.

14. Add an object composed of *timestamp* and *value* to the array *results*.

15. Execute the callback *onComplete*, passing the variables *granularityName* and *results*.

16. Make the function available as a module in Node.js. This is necessary in order to run *require("./timeseries-string")*.

The implementation of *timeseries-string* is complete. Create a file called *using-timeseries.js*, which will illustrate how to use the libraries *timeseries-string* (previously implemented) and *timeseries-hash* (to be implemented). Both of these libraries have the same API. Therefore, *using-timeseries.js* decides what library to use via a command-line argument. This file inserts data points for a *TimeSeries* instance called *item1Purchases* using hardcoded timestamps, and then it fetches values from different granularities. Before inserting data into Redis, *using-timeseries* removes all existing keys to ensure idempotency. The output will be the same with either *timeseries-string* or *timeseries-hash*:

```
var redis = require("redis");
var client = redis.createClient();

if (process.argv.length < 3) { // 1
  console.log("ERROR: You need to specify a data type!");
  console.log("$ node using-timeseries.js [string|hash]");
  process.exit(1);
}
var dataType = process.argv[2]; // 2

client.flushall(); // 3

var timeseries = require("./timeseries-" + dataType); // 4
```

```
var item1Purchases = new timeseries.TimeSeries(client,
"purchases:item1"); // 5
var beginTimestamp = 0; // 6

item1Purchases.insert(beginTimestamp); // 7
item1Purchases.insert(beginTimestamp + 1); // 8
item1Purchases.insert(beginTimestamp + 1); // 9
item1Purchases.insert(beginTimestamp + 3); // 10
item1Purchases.insert(beginTimestamp + 61); // 11

function displayResults(granularityName, results) { // 12
  console.log("Results from " + granularityName + ":");
  console.log("Timestamp \t| Value");
  console.log("--------------- | ------");
  for (var i = 0 ; i < results.length; i++) {
    console.log('\t' + results[i].timestamp + '\t| ' +
      results[i].value);
  }
  console.log();
}

item1Purchases.fetch("1sec", beginTimestamp, beginTimestamp + 4,
  displayResults); // 13

item1Purchases.fetch("1min", beginTimestamp, beginTimestamp + 120,
  displayResults); // 14

client.quit();
```

1. Check whether there are at least three arguments from the command line.

2. Assign the third argument from the command line to the variable *dataType*. The variable *process.argv* contains all the command-line arguments: the first argument is the Node.js binary path, the second is the filename, and the third is the data type name.

3. Execute the Redis command **FLUSHALL**, which removes all of the data from Redis. Use this command with caution, because this action cannot be undone.

4. Require the time series module based on the data type passed in the command line.

5. Create a *TimeSeries* object, passing the Redis client and the "purchases:item1" namespace as arguments.

6. Create the variable *beginTimestamp* and assign the timestamp 0 to it. This timestamp value was chosen to make it easier to read the output. Usually, a timestamp that represents the current time or a specific time in seconds is more useful. For instance, *Date.now() / 1000* returns the current time in seconds.

7. Execute the function *insert*, passing *beginTimestamp*.

8. Then execute the function *insert*, passing a timestamp that is 1 second after *beginTimestamp*.

9. Execute the function *insert* with the same argument as before.

10. Next, execute the function *insert*, passing a timestamp that is 3 seconds after *beginTimestamp*.

11. Execute the function *insert*, passing a timestamp that is 61 seconds after *beginTimestamp*. All calls before this line were in the same minute, but this one is in the next minute.

12. Create the function *displayResults* to display the output of a *fetch* call.

13. Execute the function *fetch* to retrieve an interval of 5 seconds in the *1sec* granularity, starting from *beginTimestamp*.

14. Execute the function *fetch* to retrieve an interval of 3 minutes in the *1min* granularity, starting from *beginTimestamp*.

Then execute the file using the following command:

```
$ node using-timeseries.js string
Results from 1sec:
Timestamp   | Value
----------- | ------
          0 | 1
          1 | 2
          2 | 0
          3 | 1
          4 | 0

Results from 1min:
Timestamp   | Value
----------- | ------
          0 | 4
         60 | 1
        120 | 0
```

This example can easily be adapted to be a stock market time series. The method *insert* will need the stock price as an additional parameter, and instead of using **INCRBY**, the method *insert* can use **SET**. The method *fetch* remains the same.

An example would be like this:

```
var stockTimeSeries = new timeseries.TimeSeries(
    client, "GOOGL");

var timestamp = (new Date(2014, 1, 28)) / 1000;

stockTimeSeries.insert(timestamp, 608.43);
```

Optimizing with Hashes

The previous time series implementation uses one Redis key for each second, minute, hour, and day. In a scenario where an event is inserted every second, there will be 87,865 keys in Redis in a full day (assuming a day starts at 00:00:00):

- 86,400 keys for the *1sec* granularity (*60 * 60 * 24*).

- 1,440 keys for the *1min* granularity (*60 * 24*).

- 24 keys for the *1hour* granularity (*24 * 1*).

- 1 key for the *1day* granularity.

This is an enormous number of keys per day, and this number grows linearly over time. A large number of keys is not very good for debugging, and each key has a memory cost that comes with it. In a benchmark test that we did—in which we inserted one event per second for 24 hours (86,400 events)—Redis allocated about 11 MB.

We can optimize this solution by using Hashes instead of Strings. Small Hashes are encoded in a different data structure, called a ziplist. This structure is memory-optimized. There are two conditions for a Hash to be encoded as a ziplist and both have to be respected:

- It must have fewer fields than the threshold Set in the configuration **hash-max-ziplist-entries**. The default value for **hash-max-ziplist-entries** is 512.

- No field value can be bigger than **hash-max-ziplist-value**. The default value for **hash-max-ziplist-value** is 64 bytes.

If any of these conditions are not met, a Hash will be converted from a ziplist to a hash table. Refer to *Chapter 1, Getting Started (The Baby Steps)*, for more information about Hashes.

The solution that we are going to present next uses about 800 KB under the same benchmark test as before.

 The benchmark used can be found at `https://gist.github.com/hltbra/2fbf5310aabbecee68c5`.

The String implementation creates at least one Redis key every time an event is inserted (unless the key was already created).

For example, an event that occurs at timestamp 0 may create the following keys:

- namespace:1sec:0
- namespace:1min:0
- namespace:1hour:0
- namespace:1day:0

If another event occurs at timestamp 1, only one more key is created (namespace:1sec:1), because it belongs to the same minute, hour, and day as timestamp 0.

In order to use Hashes and save memory space, the next solution will group multiple keys into a single Hash.

In a scenario where there is only the *1sec* granularity and there are data points across six different timestamps, the String solution will create the following keys:

Key name	Key value
namespace:1sec:0	10
namespace:1sec:1	15
namespace:1sec:2	25
namespace:1sec:3	100
namespace:1sec:4	200
namespace:1sec:5	300

In order to illustrate how to optimize the previous scenario using a Hash, groups of three keys are used:

Key name	Field name	Field value	Key name	Field name	Field value
	0	10		3	100
namespace:1sec:0	1	15	namespace:1sec:3	4	200
	2	25		5	300

The Hash implementation has the same method signatures as the String implementation. Most of the code will be the same, so we will only explain the modified lines (the changes are in bold).

Save the following code in a file called *timeseries-hash.js*:

```
function TimeSeries(client, namespace) {
  this.namespace = namespace;
  this.client = client;
  this.units = {
    second: 1,
    minute: 60,
    hour: 60 * 60,
    day: 24 * 60 * 60
  };

  this.granularities = { // 1
    '1sec'  : { name: '1sec', ttl: this.units.hour * 2,
      duration: 1, quantity: this.units.minute * 5 },
    '1min'  : { name: '1min', ttl: this.units.day * 7,
      duration: this.units.minute, quantity: this.units.hour * 8 },
    '1hour' : { name: '1hour', ttl: this.units.day * 60 ,
      duration: this.units.hour, quantity: this.units.day * 10 },
    '1day'  : { name: '1day', ttl: null, duration: this.units.day,
      quantity: this.units.day * 30 },
  };
};
```

1. The field *quantity* was added to each granularity. It is used to determine the Hash distribution:

   ° *1sec* granularity: Stores a maximum of 300 timestamps of 1 second each (5 minutes of data points)

- ○ *1min* granularity: Stores a maximum of 480 timestamps of 1 minute each (8 hours of data points)

- ○ *1hour* granularity: Stores a maximum of 240 timestamps of 1 hour each (10 days of data points)

- ○ *1day* granularity: Stores a maximum of 30 timestamps of 1 day each (30 days of data points)

The numbers were chosen based on the default Redis configuration (**hash-max-ziplist-entries** is 512), so any number smaller than 512 makes this solution more memory-efficient than the String solution. You can try new values and see how this affects memory usage with the command **INFO**. More information about the **INFO** command can be found in *Chapter 4, Commands (Where the Wild Things Are)*.

The new method *insert* follows:

```
TimeSeries.prototype.insert = function(timestampInSeconds) {
  for (var granularityName in this.granularities) {
    var granularity = this.granularities[granularityName];
    var key = this._getKeyName(granularity, timestampInSeconds);
    var fieldName = this._getRoundedTimestamp(timestampInSeconds,
      granularity.duration); // 1
    this.client.hincrby(key, fieldName, 1); // 2
    if (granularity.ttl !== null) {
      this.client.expire(key, granularity.ttl);
    }
  }
};
```

1. Create a variable *fieldName* and assign to it the proper field name, based on the granularity duration.

2. Execute the command **HINCRBY** to increment a Hash field by 1.

The new private method *_getKeyName* was changed but the private method *_getRoundedTimestamp* remained the same:

```
TimeSeries.prototype._getKeyName = function(granularity,
timestampInSeconds) {
  var roundedTimestamp = this._getRoundedTimestamp(
    timestampInSeconds, granularity.quantity); // 1
  return [this.namespace, granularity.name,
    roundedTimestamp].join(':');
};
```

```
TimeSeries.prototype._getRoundedTimestamp = function(
  timestampInSeconds, precision) {
  return Math.floor(timestampInSeconds/precision) * precision;
};
```

1. Create a timestamp that is normalized based on the granularity quantity. For instance, if *timestampInSeconds* is 2 and *granularity.quantity* is 3, *roundedTimestamp* will be 0. Here are more examples that follow the same rule:

   ○ roundedTimestamp 0 groups timestamps 0, 1, and 2

   ○ roundedTimestamp 3 groups timestamps 3, 4, and 5

   ○ roundedTimestamp 6 groups timestamps 6, 7, and 8

The new method *fetch* follows:

```
TimeSeries.prototype.fetch = function(granularityName, beginTimestamp,
endTimestamp, onComplete) {
  var granularity = this.granularities[granularityName];
  var begin = this._getRoundedTimestamp(beginTimestamp,
    granularity.duration);
  var end = this._getRoundedTimestamp(endTimestamp,
    granularity.duration);
  var fields = []; // 1
  var multi = this.client.multi(); // 2

  for (var timestamp = begin; timestamp <= end; timestamp +=
    granularity.duration) {
    var key = this._getKeyName(granularity, timestamp);
    var fieldName = this._getRoundedTimestamp(timestamp,
      granularity.duration); // 3
    multi.hget(key, fieldName); // 4
  }

  multi.exec(function(err, replies) { // 5
    var results = [];
    for (var i = 0 ; i < replies.length ; i++) {
      var timestamp = beginTimestamp + i * granularity.duration;
      var value = parseInt(replies[i], 10) || 0;
      results.push({timestamp: timestamp , value: value});
    }
```

```
    onComplete(granularityName, results);
  });
};

exports.TimeSeries = TimeSeries;
```

1. Create the variable *fields* and assign an empty array to it.

2. Create the variable *multi* and assign to it a *Multi* object that shares the same interface as *this.client*. With *multi*, commands are queued up until *multi.exec()* is executed.

3. Create the variable *fieldName* and assign the proper field name to it based on the granularity duration.

4. Execute the command **HGET** to retrieve the field value of a Hash.

5. Execute the function *multi.exec*, which executes all the queued commands in a transaction. This is used to avoid chaining of callbacks because of multiple calls to **HGET**. More details about **MULTI/EXEC** and transactions can be found in *Chapter 4, Commands (Where the Wild Things Are)*.

With this, we have completed the Hash implementation of *TimeSeries*, keeping the API and behavior the same as before.

Then execute *using-timeseries.js*, passing hash as an argument:

```
$ node using-timeseries.js hash
Results from 1sec:
Timestamp   | Value
----------- | ------
          0 | 1
          1 | 2
          2 | 0
          3 | 1
          4 | 0

Results from 1min:
Timestamp   | Value
----------- | ------
          0 | 4
         60 | 1
        120 | 0
```

Adding uniqueness with Sorted Sets and HyperLogLog

This section presents two different Time Series implementations that support unique insertions (for example, unique visitors or concurrent video plays), which are very similar to the previous solutions.

The first implementation uses Sorted Sets, and it is based on the previous Hash implementation. The second implementation uses HyperLogLog, and it is based on the previous String implementation. Since these new implementations are very similar to previous ones, only the lines highlighted in bold are explained.

Each solution has pros and cons:

- The Sorted Set solution works well and is 100% accurate
- The HyperLogLog solution uses less memory than the Sorted Set solution, but it is only 99.19% accurate

The proper solution should be chosen based on how much data needs to be stored and how accurate it needs to be.

Create a file called *timeseries-sorted-set.js*, copy the content of *timeseries-hash.js*, and change the following:

```
function TimeSeries(client, namespace) {
  this.namespace = namespace;
  this.client = client;
  this.units = {
    second: 1,
    minute: 60,
    hour: 60 * 60,
    day: 24 * 60 * 60
  };

  this.granularities = { // 1
    '1sec' : { name: '1sec', ttl: this.units.hour * 2,
      duration: 1, quantity: this.units.minute * 2 },
    '1min' : { name: '1min', ttl: this.units.day * 7,
      duration: this.units.minute, quantity: this.units.hour * 2 },
    '1hour': { name: '1hour', ttl: this.units.day * 60 ,
      duration: this.units.hour, quantity: this.units.day * 5 },
    '1day' : { name: '1day', ttl: null, duration: this.units.day,
      quantity: this.units.day * 30 },
  };
};
```

1. The field *quantity* was changed based on the Sorted Set configuration **zset-max-ziplist-entries**, which defaults to 128. *Chapter 4, Commands (Where the Wild Things Are)* has more details on this. The key distribution is as follows:

    ○ *1sec* granularity: Stores a maximum of 120 timestamps of 1 second each (2 minutes of data points)

    ○ *1min* granularity: Stores a maximum of 120 timestamps of 1 minute each (2 hours of data points)

    ○ *1hour* granularity: Stores a maximum of 120 timestamps of 1 hour each (5 days of data points)

    ○ *1day* granularity: Stores a maximum of 30 timestamps of 1 day each (30 days of data points)

The modified *insert* method is as follows:

```
TimeSeries.prototype.insert = function(timestampInSeconds, thing){ // 1
   for (var granularityName in this.granularities) {
      var granularity = this.granularities[granularityName];
      var key = this._getKeyName(granularity, timestampInSeconds);
      var timestampScore = this._getRoundedTimestamp(timestampInSeconds,
granularity.duration); // 2
      var member = timestampScore + ":" + thing; // 3
      this.client.zadd(key, timestampScore, member); // 4
      if (granularity.ttl !== null) {
        this.client.expire(key, granularity.ttl);
      }
   }
};
```

1. Modify the *insert* method to get an additional parameter, called *thing*. This parameter is the unique value to be stored (for example, user ID, username, or e-mail).

2. Rename *fieldName* to *timestampScore* to better represent the data type.

3. Create the variable *member* to be the unique value of the Sorted Set. Since Sorted Sets have unique elements, the value of *timestampScore* is prepended to the value of *thing* to avoid conflicts.

4. Execute the command **ZADD**, which adds the value of the variable *member* with the score *timestampScore* to the Sorted Set.

The modified *fetch* method is as follows:

```
TimeSeries.prototype.fetch = function(granularityName, beginTimestamp,
endTimestamp, onComplete) {
  var granularity = this.granularities[granularityName];
  var begin = this._getRoundedTimestamp(beginTimestamp, granularity.
duration);
  var end = this._getRoundedTimestamp(endTimestamp, granularity.
duration);
  var fields = [];
  var multi = this.client.multi();

  for (var timestamp = begin; timestamp <= end; timestamp +=
granularity.duration) {
    var key = this._getKeyName(granularity, timestamp);
    multi.zcount(key, timestamp, timestamp); // 1
  }

  multi.exec(function(err, replies) {
    var results = [];
    for (var i = 0 ; i < replies.length ; i++) {
      var timestamp = beginTimestamp + i * granularity.duration;
      var value = parseInt(replies[i], 10) || 0;
      results.push({timestamp: timestamp , value: value});
    }
    onComplete(granularityName, results);
  });
};
```

1. Execute the command **ZCOUNT**, which returns the number of elements in a Sorted Set in a given range of scores. It is used to retrieve the number of elements in a given timestamp.

With this, we have completed the Sorted Set implementation of *TimeSeries*.

Create a file called *using-timeseries-unique.js*, which will be very similar to *using-timeseries.js*. The main difference is the *insert* method call, which requires a string as an additional parameter (in this case, usernames of people playing videos):

```
var redis = require("redis");
var client = redis.createClient();
```

```
if (process.argv.length < 3) {
  console.log("ERROR: You need to specify a data type!");
  console.log("$ node using-timeseries.js [sorted-set|
    hyperloglog]");
  process.exit(1);
}
var dataType = process.argv[2];

client.flushall();

var timeseries = require("./timeseries-" + dataType);

var concurrentPlays = new timeseries.TimeSeries(client,
  "concurrentplays");
var beginTimestamp = 0;

concurrentPlays.insert(beginTimestamp, "user:max");
concurrentPlays.insert(beginTimestamp, "user:max");
concurrentPlays.insert(beginTimestamp + 1, "user:hugo");
concurrentPlays.insert(beginTimestamp + 1, "user:renata");
concurrentPlays.insert(beginTimestamp + 3, "user:hugo");
concurrentPlays.insert(beginTimestamp + 61, "user:kc");

function displayResults(granularityName, results) {
  console.log("Results from " + granularityName + ":");
  console.log("Timestamp \t| Value");
  console.log("--------------- | ------");
  for (var i = 0 ; i < results.length; i++) {
    console.log('\t' + results[i].timestamp + '\t| ' + results[i].
value);
  }
  console.log();
}

concurrentPlays.fetch("1sec", beginTimestamp, beginTimestamp + 4,
displayResults);

concurrentPlays.fetch("1min", beginTimestamp, beginTimestamp + 120,
displayResults);

client.quit();
```

Then execute *using-timeseries-unique.js*, passing sorted-set as an argument:

```
$ node using-timeseries-unique.js sorted-set
Results from 1sec:
Timestamp   | Value
----------- | ------
          0 | 1
          1 | 2
          2 | 0
          3 | 1
          4 | 0

Results from 1min:
Timestamp   | Value
----------- | ------
          0 | 3
         60 | 1
        120 | 0
```

The previous output showed one user for the 0 timestamp in *1sec*, although there were two inserts for the same user in that timestamp.

It also showed three users for the 0 timestamp in the *1min* granularity, although there were five entries (two repeating entries).

The HyperLogLog implementation does not perform any key grouping; it uses one key per timestamp. Compared to the String implementation, it changes the *insert* method to use **PFADD** instead of **INCRBY**, and changes the *fetch* method to make multiple calls to **PFCOUNT** instead of one call to **MGET**.

Create a file called *timeseries-hyperloglog.js*, and add the following code:

```
function TimeSeries(client, namespace) {
  this.namespace = namespace;
  this.client = client;
  this.units = {
    second: 1,
    minute: 60,
    hour: 60 * 60,
    day: 24 * 60 * 60
  };

  this.granularities = {
    '1sec' : { name: '1sec', ttl: this.units.hour * 2, duration: 1 },
```

```
    '1min' : { name: '1min', ttl: this.units.day * 7,
      duration: this.units.minute },
    '1hour': { name: '1hour', ttl: this.units.day * 60 ,
      duration: this.units.hour },
    '1day' : { name: '1day', ttl: null, duration: this.units.day }
  };
};


TimeSeries.prototype.insert = function(timestampInSeconds, thing){ // 1
  for (var granularityName in this.granularities) {
    var granularity = this.granularities[granularityName];
    var key = this._getKeyName(granularity, timestampInSeconds);
    this.client.pfadd(key, thing); // 2
    if (granularity.ttl !== null) {
      this.client.expire(key, granularity.ttl);
    }
  }
};


TimeSeries.prototype._getKeyName = function(granularity,
  timestampInSeconds) {
  var roundedTimestamp = this._getRoundedTimestamp(
    timestampInSeconds, granularity.duration);
  return [this.namespace, granularity.name,
    roundedTimestamp].join(':');
};


TimeSeries.prototype._getRoundedTimestamp = function(
  timestampInSeconds, precision) {
  return Math.floor(timestampInSeconds / precision) * precision;
};


TimeSeries.prototype.fetch = function(granularityName,
  beginTimestamp, endTimestamp, onComplete) {
  var granularity = this.granularities[granularityName];
  var begin = this._getRoundedTimestamp(beginTimestamp,
    granularity.duration);
  var end = this._getRoundedTimestamp(endTimestamp,
    granularity.duration);
  var fields = [];
  var multi = this.client.multi();

  for (var timestamp = begin; timestamp <= end; timestamp +=
    granularity.duration) {
```

```
      var key = this._getKeyName(granularity, timestamp);
      multi.pfcount(key); // 3
   }

   multi.exec(function(err, replies) {
     var results = [];
     for (var i = 0 ; i < replies.length ; i++) {
       var timestamp = beginTimestamp + i * granularity.duration;
       var value = parseInt(replies[i], 10) || 0;
       results.push({timestamp: timestamp, value: value});
     }
     onComplete(granularityName, results);
   });
};

exports.TimeSeries = TimeSeries;
```

1. Add the parameter *thing* to the method *insert*.
2. Execute the **PFADD** command to add the value of *thing* to the HyperLogLog.
3. Execute the command **PFCOUNT** to retrieve the number of elements in a given timestamp.

Summary

This chapter started with an introduction to time series with some real-world examples, and then presented different time series implementations in Node.js, using String, Hash, Sorted Set, and HyperLogLog data types.

The next chapter will introduce other Redis features, such as transactions, pipelining, Lua scripting, and administration commands, and then give more details on data type optimization.

4
Commands (Where the Wild Things Are)

This chapter gives an overview of many different Redis commands and features, from techniques to reduce network latency to extending Redis with Lua scripting.

The previous chapters briefly mentioned how to optimize data types, and at the end of this chapter, we will explain these optimizations further.

Pub/Sub

Pub/Sub stands for Publish-Subscribe, which is a pattern where messages are not sent directly to specific receivers. Publishers send messages to channels, and subscribers receive these messages if they are listening to a given channel.

Redis supports the Pub/Sub pattern and provides commands to publish messages and subscribe to channels.

Here are some examples of Pub/Sub applications:

- News and weather dashboards
- Chat applications
- Push notifications, such as subway delay alerts
- Remote code execution, similar to what the **SaltStack** tool supports

The following examples implement a remote command execution system, where a command is sent to a channel and the server that is subscribed to that channel executes the command.

The command **PUBLISH** sends a message to the Redis channel, and it returns the number of clients that received that message. A message gets lost if there are no clients subscribed to the channel when it comes in.

Create a file called *publisher.js* in the *chapter 4* folder and save the following code into it:

```
var redis = require("redis");
var client = redis.createClient();

var channel = process.argv[2]; // 1
var command = process.argv[3]; // 2

client.publish(channel, command); // 3

client.quit();
```

1. Assign the third argument from the command line to the variable *channel* (the first argument is *node* and the second is *publisher.js*).

2. Assign the fourth argument from the command line to the variable *command*.

3. Execute the command **PUBLISH**, passing the variables *channel* and *command*.

The command **SUBSCRIBE** subscribes a client to one or many channels. The command **UNSUBSCRIBE** unsubscribes a client from one or many channels.

The commands **PSUBSCRIBE** and **PUNSUBSCRIBE** work the same way as the **SUBSCRIBE** and **UNSUBSCRIBE** commands, but they accept glob-style patterns as channel names.

 Once a Redis client executes the command **SUBSCRIBE** or **PSUBSCRIBE**, it enters the subscribe mode and stops accepting commands, except for the commands **SUBSCRIBE**, **PSUBSCRIBE**, **UNSUBSCRIBE**, and **PUNSUBSCRIBE**.

Create a file called *subscriber.js* in the *chapter 4* folder and save the following:

```
var os = require("os"); // 1
var redis = require("redis");
var client = redis.createClient();

var COMMANDS = {}; // 2

COMMANDS.DATE = function() { // 3
    var now = new Date();
```

```
      console.log("DATE " + now.toISOString());
};

COMMANDS.PING = function() { // 4
  console.log("PONG");
};

COMMANDS.HOSTNAME = function() { // 5
  console.log("HOSTNAME " + os.hostname());
};

client.on("message", function(channel, commandName) { // 6
  if (COMMANDS.hasOwnProperty(commandName)) { // 7
    var commandFunction = COMMANDS[commandName]; // 8
      commandFunction(); // 9
  } else { // 10
    console.log("Unknown command: " + commandName);
  }
});
client.subscribe("global", process.argv[2]); // 11
```

1. Require the Node.js module *os*.

2. Create the variable *COMMANDS*, which is a JavaScript object. All command functions in this module will be added to this object. This object is intended to act as a namespace.

3. Create the function *DATE*, which displays the current date.

4. Then create the function *PING*, which displays **PONG**.

5. Create the function *HOSTNAME*, which displays the server hostname.

6. Register a channel listener, which is a function that executes commands based on the channel message.

7. Check whether the variable *commandName* is a valid command.

8. Create the variable *commandFunction* and assign the function to it.

9. Execute *commandFunction*.

10. Display an error message if the variable *commandName* contains a command that is not available.

11. Execute the command **SUBSCRIBE**, passing "*global*", which is the channel that all clients subscribe to, and a channel name from the command line.

Open three terminal windows and run the previous files, as shown the following screenshot (from left to right and top to bottom):

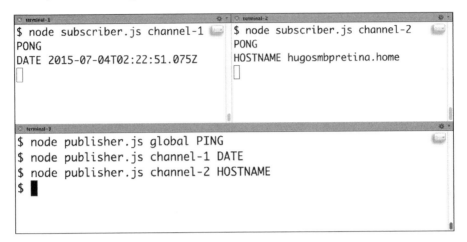

- **terminal-1**: A subscriber that listens to the global channel and **channel-1**
- **terminal-2**: A subscriber that listens to the global channel and **channel-2**
- **terminal-3**: A publisher that publishes the message **PING** to the global channel (both subscribers receive the message), the message **DATE** to channel-1 (the first subscriber receives it), and the message **HOSTNAME** to **channel-2** (the second subscriber receives it)

The command **PUBSUB** introspects the state of the Redis Pub/Sub system. This command accepts three subcommands: CHANNELS, NUMSUB, and NUMPAT.

The CHANNELS subcommand returns all active channels (channels with at least one subscriber). This command accepts an optional parameter, which is a glob-style pattern. If the pattern is specified, all channel names that match the pattern are returned; if no pattern is specified, all channel names are returned. The command syntax is as follows:

```
PUBSUB CHANNELS [pattern]
```

The NUMSUB subcommand returns the number of clients connected to channels via the **SUBSCRIBE** command. This command accepts many channel names as arguments. Its syntax is as follows:

```
PUBSUB NUMSUB [channel-1 ... channel-N]
```

The NUMPAT subcommand returns the number of clients connected to channels via the **PSUBSCRIBE** command. This command does not accept channel patterns as arguments. Its syntax is as follows:

```
PUBSUB NUMPAT
```

 Redis contributor *Pieter Noordhuis* created a web chat implementation in Ruby using Redis and Pub/Sub. It can be found at `https://gist.github.com/pietern/348262`.

Transactions

A transaction in Redis is a sequence of commands executed in order and atomically. The command **MULTI** marks the beginning of a transaction, and the command **EXEC** marks its end. Any commands between the **MULTI** and **EXEC** commands are serialized and executed as an atomic operation. Redis does not serve any other client in the middle of a transaction.

All commands in a transaction are queued in the client and are only sent to the server when the **EXEC** command is executed. It is possible to prevent a transaction from being executed by using the **DISCARD** command instead of **EXEC**. Usually, Redis clients prevent a transaction from being sent to Redis if it contains command syntax errors.

Unlike in traditional SQL databases, transactions in Redis are not rolled back if they produce failures. Redis executes the commands in order, and if any of them fail, it proceeds to the next command. Another downside of Redis transactions is that it is not possible to make any decisions inside the transaction, since all the commands are queued.

For example, the following code simulates a bank transfer. Here, money is transferred from a source account to a destination account inside a Redis transaction. If the source account has enough funds, the transaction is executed. Otherwise, it is discarded.

Save the following code in a file called *bank-transaction.js* in the *chapter 4* folder:

```
var redis = require("redis");
var client = redis.createClient();

function transfer(from, to, value, callback) { // 1
  client.get(from, function(err, balance) { // 2
    var multi = client.multi(); // 3
    multi.decrby(from, value); // 4
    multi.incrby(to, value); // 5
```

```
      if (balance >= value) { // 6
        multi.exec(function(err, reply) { // 7
          callback(null, reply[0]); // 8
        });
      } else {
        multi.discard(); // 9
        callback(new Error("Insufficient funds"), null); // 10
      }
    });
  }
```

1. Create the function *transfer*, which receives an account ID from which to withdraw money, another account ID from which to receive money, the monetary value to transfer, and a callback function to call after the transfer.

2. Retrieve the current balance of the source account.

3. Create a *Multi* object, which represents the transaction. All commands sent to it are queued and executed after the **EXEC** command is issued.

4. Enqueue the command **DECRBY** into the *Multi* object.

5. Then enqueue the command **INCRBY** into the *Multi* object.

6. Check whether the source account has sufficient funds.

7. Execute the **EXEC** command, which triggers sequential execution of the queued transaction commands.

8. Execute the callback function and pass the value *null* as an error, and the balance of the source account after the command **DECRBY** is executed.

9. Execute the **DISCARD** command to discard the transaction. No commands from the transaction will be executed in Redis.

10. Execute the function *callback* and pass an error object if the source account has insufficient funds.

The following code uses the previous example, transferring $40 from Max's account to Hugo's account (both accounts had $100 before the transfer).

Append the following to the file *bank-transaction.js*:

```
client.mset("max:checkings", 100, "hugo:checkings", 100, function(err,
reply) { // 1
  console.log("Max checkings: 100");
  console.log("Hugo checkings: 100");
  transfer("max:checkings", "hugo:checkings", 40,
    function(err, balance) { // 2
```

```
      if (err) {
        console.log(err);
      } else {
        console.log("Transferred 40 from Max to Hugo")
        console.log("Max balance:", balance);
      }
      client.quit();
    });
  });
```

1. Set the initial balance of each account to $100.

2. Execute the function *transfer* to transfer $40 from *max:checkings* to *hugo:checkings*.

Then execute the file using the following command:

```
$ node bank-transaction.js
Max checkings: 100
Hugo checkings: 100
Transferred 40 from Max to Hugo
Max balance: 60
```

It is possible to make the execution of a transaction conditional using the **WATCH** command, which implements an optimistic lock on a group of keys. The **WATCH** command marks keys as being watched so that **EXEC** executes the transaction only if the keys being watched were not changed. Otherwise, it returns a *null* reply and the operation needs to be repeated; this is the reason it is called an optimistic lock. The command **UNWATCH** removes keys from the watch list.

The following code implements a *zpop* function, which removes the first element of a Sorted Set and passes it to a callback function, using a transaction with **WATCH**. A race condition could exist if the **WATCH** command is not used.

Create a file called *watch-transaction.js* in the *chapter 4* folder with the following code:

```
var redis = require("redis");
var client = redis.createClient();

function zpop(key, callback) { // 1
  client.watch(key, function(watchErr, watchReply) { // 2
    client.zrange(key, 0, 0, function(zrangeErr, zrangeReply) { // 3
      var multi = client.multi(); // 4
      multi.zrem(key, zrangeReply); // 5
      multi.exec(function(transactionErr, transactionReply) { // 6
        if (transactionReply) {
```

```
            callback(zrangeReply[0]); // 7
        } else {
            zpop(key, callback); // 8
        }
    });
  });
 });
}
client.zadd("presidents", 1732, "George Washington");
client.zadd("presidents", 1809, "Abraham Lincoln");
client.zadd("presidents", 1858, "Theodore Roosevelt");

zpop("presidents", function(member) {
  console.log("The first president in the group is:", member);
  client.quit();
});
```

1. Create the function *zpop*, which receives a key and a callback function as arguments.

2. Execute the **WATCH** command on the key passed as an argument.

3. Then execute the **ZRANGE** command to retrieve the first element of the Sorted Set.

4. Create a *multi* object.

5. Enqueue the **ZREM** command in the transaction.

6. Execute the transaction.

7. Execute the *callback* function if the key being watched has not been changed.

8. Execute the function *zpop* with the same parameters as before if the key being watched has not been changed.

Then execute the file using the following command:

```
$ node watch-transaction.js
The first president in the group is: George Washington
```

Pipelines

In Redis, a pipeline is a way to send multiple commands together to the Redis server without waiting for individual replies. The replies are read all at once by the client. The time taken for a Redis client to send a command and obtain a reply from the Redis server is called **Round Trip Time (RTT)**. When multiple commands are sent, there are multiple RTTs.

Pipelines can decrease the number of RTTs because commands are grouped, so a pipeline with 10 commands will have only one RTT. This can improve the network's performance significantly.

For instance, if the network link between a client and server has an RTT of 100 ms, the maximum number of commands that can be sent per second is 10, no matter how many commands can be handled by the Redis server. Usually, a Redis server can handle hundreds of thousands of commands per second, and not using pipelines may be a waste of resources.

When Redis is used without pipelines, each command needs to wait for a reply. Assume the following:

```
var redis = require("redis");
var client = redis.createClient();

client.set("key1", "value1");
client.set("key2", "value2");
client.set("key3", "value3");
```

Three separate commands are sent to Redis, and each command waits for its reply. The following diagram shows what happens when Redis is used without pipelines:

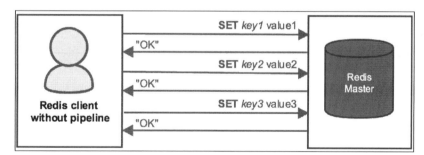

Redis commands sent in a pipeline must be independent. They run sequentially in the server (the order is preserved), but they do not run as a transaction. Even though pipelines are neither transactional nor atomic (this means that different Redis commands may occur between the ones in the pipeline), they are still useful because they can save a lot of network time, preventing the network from becoming a bottleneck as it often does with heavy load applications.

By default, *node_redis*, the Node.js library we are using, sends commands in pipelines and automatically chooses how many commands will go into each pipeline. Therefore, you don't need to worry about this. However, other Redis clients may not use pipelines by default; you will need to check out the client documentation to see how to take advantage of pipelines. The PHP, Python, and Ruby clients presented in *Chapter 5, Clients for Your Favorite Language (Become a Redis Polyglot)*, do not use pipelines by default.

This is what happens when commands are sent to Redis in a pipeline:

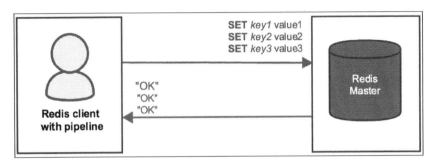

 When sending many commands, it might be a good idea to use multiple pipelines rather than one big pipeline.

Pipelines are not a new idea or an exclusive feature or command in Redis; they are just a technique of sending a group of commands to a server at once.

Commands inside a transaction may not be sent as a pipeline by default. This will depend on the Redis client you are using. For example, *node_redis* sends everything automatically in pipelines (as we mentioned before), but different clients may require additional configuration. It is a good idea to send transactions in a pipeline to avoid an extra round trip.

Scripting

Redis 2.6 introduced the scripting feature, and the language that was chosen to extend Redis was Lua. Before Redis 2.6, there was only one way to extend Redis— changing its source code, which was written in C.

Lua was chosen because it is very small and simple, and its C API is very easy to integrate with other libraries. Although it is lightweight, Lua is a very powerful language (it is commonly used in game development).

Lua scripts are atomically executed, which means that the Redis server is blocked during script execution. Because of this, Redis has a default timeout of 5 seconds to run any script, although this value can be changed through the configuration **lua-time-limit**.

Redis will not automatically terminate a Lua script when it times out. Instead, it will start to reply with a **BUSY** message to every command, stating that a script is running. The only way to make the server return to normalcy is by aborting the script execution with the command **SCRIPT KILL** or **SHUTDOWN NOSAVE**.

Ideally, scripts should be simple, have a single responsibility, and run fast.

 The popular games Civilization V, Angry Birds, and World of Warcraft use Lua as their scripting language.

Lua syntax basics

Lua is built around basic types such as booleans, numbers, strings, tables (the only composite data type), and functions.

Let's see some basics of Lua's syntax:

- Comments:

  ```
  -- this is a comment
  ```

- Global variable declaration:

  ```
  x = 123
  ```

- Local variable declaration:

  ```
  local y = 456
  ```

- Function definition:

  ```
  function hello_world()
     return "Hello World"
  end
  ```

- Iteration:

  ```
  for i = 1, 10 do
      print(i)
  end
  ```

- Conditionals:

```
if x == 123 then
  print("x is the magic number")
else
  print("I have no idea what x is")
end
```

- String concatenation:

```
print("Hello" .. " World")
```

- Using a table as an array — arrays in Lua start indexing at 1, not at 0 (as in most languages):

```
data_types = {1.0, 123, "redis", true, false, hello_world}
print(data_types[3]) -- the output is "redis"
```

- Using a table as a hash:

```
languages = {lua = 1993, javascript = 1995, python = 1991, ruby = 1995}
print("Lua was created in " .. languages["lua"])
print("JavaScript was created in " .. languages.javascript)
```

Redis meets Lua

A Redis client must send Lua scripts as strings to the Redis server. Therefore, this section will have JavaScript strings that contain Lua code.

Redis can evaluate any valid Lua code, and a few libraries are available (for example, bitop, cjson, math, and string). There are also two functions that execute Redis commands: *redis.call* and *redis.pcall*. The function *redis.call* requires the command name and all its parameters, and it returns the result of the executed command. If there are errors, *redis.call* aborts the script. The function *redis.pcall* is similar to *redis.call*, but in the event of an error, it returns the error as a Lua table and continues the script execution. Every script can return a value through the keyword *return*, and if there is no explicit return, the value *nil* is returned.

It is possible to pass Redis key names and parameters to a Lua script, and they will be available inside the Lua script through the variables *KEYS* and *ARGV*, respectively.

Both *redis.call* and *redis.pcall* automatically convert the result of a Redis command to a Lua type, which means that if the Redis command returns an integer, it will be converted into a Lua number. The same thing happens to commands that return a string or an array. Since every script will return a value, this value will be converted from a Lua type to a Redis type.

There are two commands for running Lua scripts: **EVAL** and **EVALSHA**. The next example will use **EVAL**, and its syntax is the following:

```
EVAL script numkeys key [key ...] arg [arg ...]
```

The parameters are as follows:

- *script*: The Lua script itself, as a string
- *numkeys*: The number of Redis keys being passed as parameters to the script
- *key*: The key name that will be available through the variable *KEYS* inside the script
- *arg*: An additional argument that will be available through the variable *ARGV* inside the script

The following code uses Lua to run the command **GET** and retrieve a key value. Create a file called *intro-lua.js* in the *chapter 4* folder with the following code:

```
var redis = require("redis");
var client = redis.createClient();

client.set("mykey", "myvalue"); // 1

var luaScript = 'return redis.call("GET", KEYS[1])'; // 2
client.eval(luaScript, 1, "mykey", function(err, reply) { // 3
  console.log(reply); // 4
  client.quit();
});
```

1. Execute the command **SET** to create a key called mykey.
2. Create the variable *luaScript* and assign the Lua code to it. This Lua code uses the *redis.call* function to execute the Redis command **GET**, passing a parameter. The *KEYS* variable is an array with all key names passed to the script.
3. Execute the command **EVAL** to execute a Lua script.
4. Display the return of the Lua script execution.

Then execute it:

```
$ node intro-lua.js
myvalue
```

 Avoid using hardcoded key names inside a Lua script; pass all key names as parameters to the commands **EVAL/EVALSHA**.

Previously in this chapter, in the *Transactions* section, we presented an implementation of a *zpop* function using **WATCH/MULTI/EXEC**. That implementation was based on an optimistic lock, which meant that the entire operation had to be retried if a client changed the Sorted Set before the **MULTI/EXEC** was executed.

The same *zpop* function can be implemented as a Lua script, and it will be simpler and atomic, which means that retries will not be necessary. Redis will always guarantee that there are no parallel changes to the Sorted Set during script execution.

Create a file called *zpop-lua.js* in the *chapter 4* folder and save the following code into it:

```
var redis = require("redis");
var client = redis.createClient();

client.zadd("presidents", 1732, "George Washington");
client.zadd("presidents", 1809, "Abraham Lincoln");
client.zadd("presidents", 1858, "Theodore Roosevelt");

var luaScript = [
  'local elements = redis.call("ZRANGE", KEYS[1], 0, 0)',
  'redis.call("ZREM", KEYS[1], elements[1])',
  'return elements[1]'
].join('\n'); // 1

client.eval(luaScript, 1, "presidents", function(err, reply){ // 2
  console.log("The first president in the group is:", reply);
  client.quit();
});
```

1. Create the variable *luaScript* and assign the Lua code to it. This Lua code uses the *redis.call* function to execute the Redis command **ZRANGE** to retrieve an array with only the first element in the Sorted Set. Then, it executes the command **ZREM** to remove the first element of the Sorted Set, before returning the removed element.

2. Execute the command **EVAL** to execute a Lua script.

Then, execute the file using the following command:

```
$ node zpop-lua.js
The first president in the group is: George Washington
```

 Many Redis users have replaced their transactional code in the form of **WATCH/MULTI/EXEC** with Lua scripts.

It is possible to save network bandwidth usage by using the commands **SCRIPT LOAD** and **EVALSHA** instead of **EVAL** when executing the same script multiple times. The command **SCRIPT LOAD** caches a Lua script and returns an identifier (which is the SHA1 hash of the script). The command **EVALSHA** executes a Lua script based on an identifier returned by **SCRIPT LOAD**. With **EVALSHA**, only a small identifier is transferred over the network, rather than a Lua code snippet:

```
var redis = require("redis");
var client = redis.createClient();

var luaScript = 'return "Lua script using EVALSHA"';
client.script("load", luaScript, function(err, reply) {
  var scriptId = reply;

  client.evalsha(scriptId, 0, function(err, reply) {
    console.log(reply);
    client.quit();
  })
});
```

Then execute the script:

```
$ node zpop-lua-evalsha.js
Lua script using EVALSHA
```

In order to make scripts play nicely with Redis replication, you should write scripts that do not change Redis keys in non-deterministic ways (that is, do not use random values). Well-written scripts behave the same way when they are re-executed with the same data. Redis replication will be explained in *Chapter 8, Scaling Redis (Beyond a Single Instance)*.

Miscellaneous commands

This section covers the most important Redis commands that we have not previously explained. These commands are very helpful in a variety of situations, including obtaining a list of clients connected to the server, monitoring the health of a Redis server, expiring keys, and migrating keys to a remote server. All the examples in this section use **redis-cli**.

INFO

The **INFO** command returns all Redis server statistics, including information about the Redis version, operating system, connected clients, memory usage, persistence, replication, and keyspace. By default, the **INFO** command shows all available sections: memory, persistence, CPU, command, cluster, clients, and replication. You can also restrict the output by specifying the section name as a parameter:

```
127.0.0.1:6379> INFO memory
# Memory
used_memory:354923856
used_memory_human:338.48M
used_memory_rss:468979712
used_memory_peak:423014496
used_memory_peak_human:403.42M
used_memory_lua:33792
mem_fragmentation_ratio:1.32
mem_allocator:libc


127.0.0.1:6379> INFO cpu
# CPU
used_cpu_sys:3.71
used_cpu_user:40.36
used_cpu_sys_children:0.00
used_cpu_user_children:0.00
```

DBSIZE

The **DBSIZE** command returns the number of existing keys in a Redis server:

```
127.0.0.1:6379> DBSIZE
(integer) 50
```

DEBUG SEGFAULT

The **DEBUG SEGFAULT** command crashes the Redis server process by performing an invalid memory access. It can be quite interesting to simulate bugs during the development of your application:

```
127.0.0.1:6379> DEBUG SEGFAULT
```

MONITOR

The command **MONITOR** shows all the commands processed by the Redis server in real time. It can be helpful for seeing how busy a Redis server is:

```
127.0.0.1:6379> MONITOR
```

The following screenshot shows the **MONITOR** command output (left side) after running the *leaderboard.js* example (right side):

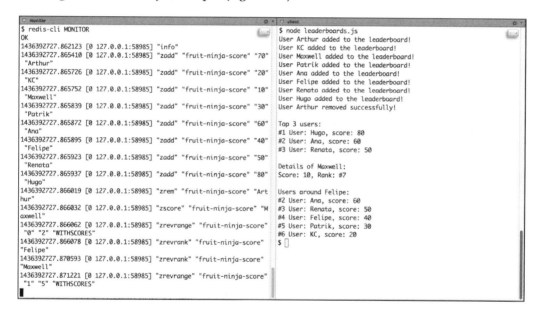

While the **MONITOR** command is very helpful for debugging, it has a cost. In the Redis documentation page for **MONITOR,** an unscientific benchmark test says that **MONITOR** could reduce Redis's throughput by over 50%.

CLIENT LIST and CLIENT SET NAME

The **CLIENT LIST** command returns a list of all clients connected to the server, as well as relevant information and statistics about the clients (for example, IP address, name, and idle time).

The **CLIENT SETNAME** command changes a client name; it is only useful for debugging purposes.

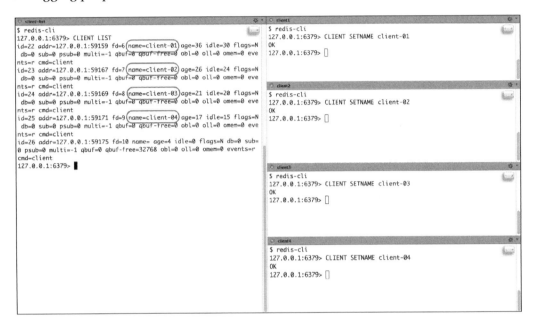

CLIENT KILL

The **CLIENT KILL** command terminates a client connection. It is possible to terminate client connections by IP, port, ID, or type:

```
127.0.0.1:6379> CLIENT KILL ADDR 127.0.0.1:51167
(integer) 1
127.0.0.1:6379> CLIENT KILL ID 22
(integer) 1
127.0.0.1:6379> CLIENT KILL TYPE slave
(integer) 0
```

FLUSHALL

The **FLUSHALL** command deletes all keys from Redis — this cannot be undone:

```
127.0.0.1:6379> FLUSHALL
OK
```

RANDOMKEY

The command **RANDOMKEY** returns a random existing key name. This may help you get an overview of the available keys in Redis. The alternative would be to run the **KEYS** command, but it analyzes all the existing keys in Redis. If the keyspace is large, it may block the Redis server entirely during its execution:

```
127.0.0.1:6379> RANDOMKEY
"mykey"
```

EXPIRE and EXPIREAT

The command **EXPIRE** sets a timeout in seconds for a given key. The key will be deleted after the specified amount of seconds. A negative timeout will delete the key instantaneously (just like running the command **DEL**).

The command **EXPIREAT** sets a timeout for a given key based on a Unix timestamp. A timestamp of the past will delete the key instantaneously.

These commands return *1* if the key timeout is set successfully or *0* if the key does not exist:

```
127.0.0.1:6379> MSET key1 value1 key2 value2
OK
127.0.0.1:6379> EXPIRE key1 30
(integer) 1
127.0.0.1:6379> EXPIREAT key2 1435717600
(integer) 1
```

TTL and PTTL

The **TTL** command returns the remaining time to live (in seconds) of a key that has an associated timeout. If the key does not have an associated **TTL**, it returns *-1*, and if the key does not exist, it returns *-2*. The **PTTL** command does the same thing, but the return value is in milliseconds rather than seconds:

```
127.0.0.1:6379> SET redis-essentials:authors "By Maxwell Dayvson da Silva, Hugo
Lopes Tavares" EX 30
```

```
OK
127.0.0.1:6379> TTL redis-essentials:authors
(integer) 18
127.0.0.1:6379> PTTL redis-essentials:authors
(integer) 13547
```

The **SET** command has optional parameters, and these were not shown before. The complete command syntax is as follows:

```
SET key value [EX seconds|PX milliseconds] [NX|XX]
```

The parameters are explained as follows:

- EX: Set an expiration time in seconds
- PX: Set an expiration time in milliseconds
- NX: Only set the key if it does not exist
- XX: Only set the key if it already exists

PERSIST

The **PERSIST** command removes the existing timeout of a given key. Such a key will never expire, unless a new timeout is set. It returns *1* if the timeout is removed or *0* if the key does not have an associated timeout:

```
127.0.0.1:6379> SET mykey value
OK
127.0.0.1:6379> EXPIRE mykey 30
(integer) 1
127.0.0.1:6379> PERSIST mykey
(integer) 1
127.0.0.1:6379> TTL mykey
(integer) -1
```

SETEX

The **SETEX** command sets a value to a given key and also sets an expiration atomically. It is a combination of the commands, **SET** and **EXPIRE**:

```
127.0.0.1:6379> SETEX mykey 30 value
OK
127.0.0.1:6379> GET mykey
"value"
127.0.0.1:6379> TTL mykey
(integer) 29
```

DEL

The **DEL** command removes one or many keys from Redis and returns the number of removed keys—this command cannot be undone:

```
127.0.0.1:6379> MSET key1 value1 key2 value2
OK
127.0.0.1:6379> DEL key1 key2
(integer) 2
```

EXISTS

The **EXISTS** command returns *1* if a certain key exists and *0* if it does not:

```
127.0.0.1:6379> SET mykey myvalue
OK
127.0.0.1:6379> EXISTS mykey
(integer) 1
```

PING

The **PING** command returns the string "**PONG**". It is useful for testing a server/client connection and verifying that Redis is able to exchange data:

```
127.0.0.1:6379> PING
PONG
```

MIGRATE

The **MIGRATE** command moves a given key to a destination Redis server. This is an atomic command, and during the key migration, both Redis servers are blocked. If the key already exists in the destination, this command fails (unless the REPLACE parameter is specified).

The command syntax is as follows:

```
MIGRATE host port key destination-db timeout [COPY] [REPLACE]
```

There are two optional parameters for the command **MIGRATE**, which can be used separately or combined:

- **COPY**: Keep the key in the local Redis server and create a copy in the destination Redis server
- **REPLACE**: Replace the existing key in the destination server

SELECT

Redis has a concept of multiple databases, each of which is identified by a number from 0 to 15 (there are 16 databases by default). It is not recommended to use multiple databases with Redis. A better approach would be to use multiple **redis-server** processes rather than a single one, because multiple processes are able to use multiple CPU cores and give better insights into bottlenecks.

The **SELECT** command changes the current database that the client is connected to. The default database is *0*:

```
127.0.0.1:6379> SELECT 7
OK
127.0.0.1:6379[7]>
```

AUTH

The **AUTH** command is used to authorize a client to connect to Redis. If authorization is enabled on the Redis server, clients are allowed to run commands only after executing the **AUTH** command with the right authorization key. More details on how to configure authorization and other security techniques are presented in *Chapter 7, Security Techniques (Guard Your Data)*:

```
127.0.0.1:6379> GET mykey
(error) NOAUTH Authentication required.
127.0.0.1:6379> AUTH mysecret
OK
127.0.0.1:6379> GET mykey
"value"
```

SCRIPT KILL

The **SCRIPT KILL** command terminates the running Lua script if no write operations have been performed by the script. If the script has performed any write operations, the **SCRIPT KILL** command will not be able to terminate it; in that case, the **SHUTDOWN NOSAVE** command must be executed.

There are three possible return values for this command:

- **OK**
- **NOTBUSY No scripts in execution right now.**
- **UNKILLABLE Sorry the script already executed write commands against the dataset. You can either wait the script termination or kill the server in a hard way using the SHUTDOWN NOSAVE command.**

```
127.0.0.1:6379> SCRIPT KILL
OK
```

SHUTDOWN

The **SHUTDOWN** command stops all clients, causes data to persist if enabled, and shuts down the Redis server.

This command accepts one of the following optional parameters:

- **SAVE**: Forces Redis to save all of the data to a file called *dump.rdb*, even if persistence is not enabled
- **NOSAVE**: Prevents Redis from persisting data to the disk, even if persistence is enabled

```
127.0.0.1:6379> SHUTDOWN SAVE
not connected>
127.0.0.1:6379> SHUTDOWN NOSAVE
not connected>
```

OBJECT ENCODING

The **OBJECT ENCODING** command returns the encoding used by a given key:

```
127.0.0.1:6379> HSET myhash field value
(integer) 1
127.0.0.1:6379> OBJECT ENCODING myhash
"ziplist"
```

Data type optimizations

In Redis, all data types can use different encodings to save memory or improve performance. For instance, a String that has only digits (for example, *12345*) uses less memory than a string of letters (for example, *abcde*) because they use different encodings. Data types will use different encodings based on thresholds defined in the Redis server configuration.

 The **redis-cli** will be used in this section to inspect the encodings of each data type and to demonstrate how configurations can be tweaked to optimize for memory.

When Redis is downloaded, it comes with a file called *redis.conf*. This file is well documented and has all the Redis configuration directives, although some of them are commented out. Usually, the default values in this file are sufficient for most applications. The Redis configurations can also be specified via the command-line option or the **CONFIG** command; the most common approach is to use a configuration file.

For this section, we have decided to not use a Redis configuration file. The configurations are passed via the command line for simplicity.

Start **redis-server** with low values for all configurations:

```
$ redis-server --hash-max-ziplist-entries 3 --hash-max-ziplist-value 5
--list-max-ziplist-entries 3 --list-max-ziplist-value 5 --set-max-intset-
entries 3 --zset-max-ziplist-entries 3 --zset-max-ziplist-value 5
```

 The default *redis.conf* file is well documented, and we recommend that you read it and discover new directive configurations.

String

The following are the available encoding for Strings:

- *int*: This is used when the string is represented by a 64-bit signed integer
- *embstr*: This is used for strings with fewer than 40 bytes
- *raw*: This is used for strings with more than 40 bytes

These encodings are not configurable. The following **redis-cli** examples show how the different encodings are chosen:

```
127.0.0.1:6379> SET str1 12345
OK
127.0.0.1:6379> OBJECT ENCODING str1
"int"
127.0.0.1:6379> SET str2 "An embstr is small"
OK
127.0.0.1:6379> OBJECT ENCODING str2
"embstr"
127.0.0.1:6379> SET str3 "A raw encoded String is anything greater than 39
bytes"
OK
127.0.0.1:6379> OBJECT ENCODING str3
"raw"
```

List

These are the available encodings for Lists:

- **ziplist**: This is used when the List size has fewer elements than the configuration **list-max-ziplist-entries** and each List element has fewer bytes than the configuration **list-max-ziplist-value**
- **linkedlist**: This is used when the previous limits are exceeded

```
127.0.0.1:6379> LPUSH list1 a b
(integer) 2
127.0.0.1:6379> OBJECT ENCODING list1
"ziplist"
127.0.0.1:6379> LPUSH list2 a b c d
(integer) 4
127.0.0.1:6379> OBJECT ENCODING list2
"linkedlist"
127.0.0.1:6379> LPUSH list3 "only one element"
(integer) 1
127.0.0.1:6379> OBJECT ENCODING list3
"linkedlist"
```

Set

The following are the available encodings for Sets:

- **intset**: This is used when all elements of a Set are integers and the Set cardinality is smaller than the configuration **set-max-intset-entries**
- **hashtable**: This is used when any element of a Set is not an integer or the Set cardinality exceeds the configuration **set-max-intset-entries**

```
127.0.0.1:6379> SADD set1 1 2
(integer) 2
127.0.0.1:6379> OBJECT ENCODING set1
"intset"
127.0.0.1:6379> SADD set2 1 2 3 4 5
(integer) 5
127.0.0.1:6379> OBJECT ENCODING set2
"hashtable"
127.0.0.1:6379> SADD set3 a
(integer) 1
127.0.0.1:6379> OBJECT ENCODING set3
"hashtable"
```

Hash

The following are the available encodings for Hashes:

- **ziplist**: Used when the number of fields in the Hash does not exceed the configuration **hash-max-ziplist-entries** and each field name and value of the Hash is less than the configuration **hash-max-ziplist-value** (in bytes).

- **hashtable**: Used when a Hash size or any of its values exceed the configurations **hash-max-ziplist-entries** and **hash-max-ziplist-value**, respectively:

```
127.0.0.1:6379> HMSET myhash1 a 1 b 2
OK
127.0.0.1:6379> OBJECT ENCODING myhash1
"ziplist"
127.0.0.1:6379> HMSET myhash2 a 1 b 2 c 3 d 4 e 5 f 6
OK
127.0.0.1:6379> OBJECT ENCODING myhash2
"hashtable"
127.0.0.1:6379> HMSET myhash3 a 1 b 2 c 3 d 4 e 5 f 6
OK
127.0.0.1:6379> OBJECT ENCODING myhash3
"hashtable"
```

Sorted Set

The following are the available encodings:

- **ziplist**: Used when a Sorted Set has fewer entries than the configuration **set-max-ziplist-entries** and each of its values are smaller than **zset-max-ziplist-value** (in bytes)

- **skiplist and hashtable**: These are used when the Sorted Set number of entries or size of any of its values exceed the configurations **set-max-ziplist-entries** and **zset-max-ziplist-value**

```
127.0.0.1:6379> ZADD zset1 1 a
(integer) 1
127.0.0.1:6379> OBJECT ENCODING zset1
"ziplist"
127.0.0.1:6379> ZADD zset2 1 abcdefghij
```

```
(integer) 1
127.0.0.1:6379> OBJECT ENCODING zset2
"skiplist"
127.0.0.1:6379> ZADD zset3 1 a 2 b 3 c 4 d
(integer) 4
127.0.0.1:6379> OBJECT ENCODING zset3
"skiplist"
```

Measuring memory usage

Previously, **redis-server** was configured to use a ziplist for Hashes with a
maximum of three elements, in which each element was smaller than 5 bytes.
With that configuration, it was possible to check how much memory Redis
would use to store 500 field-value pairs:

```
$ redis-cli FLUSHALL
OK
$ redis-cli INFO memory
# Memory
used_memory:1008576    before
used_memory_human:984.94K
used_memory_rss:1851392
used_memory_peak:1008576
used_memory_peak_human:984.94K
used_memory_lua:36864
mem_fragmentation_ratio:1.84
mem_allocator:libc
$ pairs=""
$ for i in {1..500} ; do pairs="$pairs field-name-$i field-value-$i" ; done
$ redis-cli HMSET hash $pairs
OK
$ redis-cli INFO memory
# Memory
used_memory:1076864    after
used_memory_human:1.03M
used_memory_rss:1994752
used_memory_peak:1076864
used_memory_peak_human:1.03M
used_memory_lua:36864
mem_fragmentation_ratio:1.85
mem_allocator:libc
$
```

The total used memory was approximately 68 kB (1,076,864 – 1,008,576 = 68,288 bytes).

If **redis-server** was started with its default configuration of 512 elements and 64 bytes for **hash-max-ziplist-entries** and **hash-max-ziplist-value**, respectively, the same 500 field-value pairs would use less memory, as shown here:

```
$ redis-cli FLUSHALL
OK
$ redis-cli INFO memory
# Memory
used_memory:1008624   before
used_memory_human:984.98K
used_memory_rss:1822720
used_memory_peak:1008624
used_memory_peak_human:984.98K
used_memory_lua:36864
mem_fragmentation_ratio:1.81
mem_allocator:libc
$ pairs=""
$ for i in {1..500} ; do pairs="$pairs field-name-$i field-value-$i" ; done
$ redis-cli HMSET hash $pairs
OK
$ redis-cli INFO memory
# Memory
used_memory:1025104   after
used_memory_human:1001.08K
used_memory_rss:1945600
used_memory_peak:1025104
used_memory_peak_human:1001.08K
used_memory_lua:36864
mem_fragmentation_ratio:1.90
mem_allocator:libc
$
```

The total used memory is approximately 16 kB (1,025,104 – 1,008,624 = 16,480 bytes). The default configuration in this case was more than four times more memory-efficient.

Forcing a Hash to be a ziplist has a trade-off—the more elements a Hash has, the slower the performance. A ziplist is a dually linked list designed to be memory-efficient, and lookups are performed in linear time ($O(n)$, where n is the number of fields in a Hash). On the other hand, a hashtable's lookup runs in constant time ($O(1)$), no matter how many elements exist.

If you have a large dataset and need to optimize for memory, tweak these configurations until you find a good trade-off between memory and performance. *Chapter 1, Getting Started (The Baby Steps)*, mentioned that Instagram tweaked their Hash configurations and found that 1,000 elements per Hash was a good trade-off for them. You can learn more about the Instagram solution in the blog post at `http://instagram-engineering.tumblr.com/post/12202313862/storing-hundreds-of-millions-of-simple-key-value`.

The same logic for tweaking configurations and trade-offs applies to all other data type encodings presented previously.

 Algorithms that run in linear time ($O(n)$) are not always bad. If the input size is very small, they can run in near-constant time.

Summary

This chapter introduced the concepts behind Pub/Sub, transactions, and pipelines. It also showed the basics of the Lua language syntax, along with explanations on how to extend Redis with Lua.

A good variety of Redis commands was presented, such as commands that are used to monitor and debug a Redis server.

This chapter also showed how to perform data type optimizations by tweaking the **redis-server** configuration.

In the next chapter, we will introduce Redis clients for languages such as PHP, Python, and Ruby.

5
Clients for Your Favorite Language (Become a Redis Polyglot)

So far in this book, we have used two Redis clients: **redis-cli** and **node_redis**.

Redis has client libraries for pretty much all the popular programming languages, and this chapter covers other Redis client libraries for PHP, Python, and Ruby.

This chapter does not provide explanations about each languages' syntax. Its main goal is to give you a better understanding of how clients in other languages work. Unlike the Node.js client used in the previous chapters, the chosen clients for PHP, Python, and Ruby are synchronous and do not require a callback function.

Most clients have a very straightforward interface to execute most of Redis commands. As long as you know how to execute a command using **redis-cli** or **node_redis**, there are high chances that you know how to use other clients in your favorite language.

This chapter will show how to use blocking commands, transactions, pipelines, and scripting. These commands are not as simple as most other commands, and their implementation varies more frequently. The most basic commands will not be covered in detail (for example, **GET**, **SET**, **INCR**, **HSET**, **SADD**, and **ZADD**).

PHP

This section shows how to use a client called *Predis*, which is the PHP Redis client recommended by the community—although there are more than 10 open source Redis clients for PHP. The PHP version used to run all examples is 5.4.

Predis can be installed in many ways, and we have decided to use PHP Composer.

Create a file called *composer.json* in the *chapter 5* folder with the following content:

```
{
    "name": "redis/chapter5",
    "require": {
        "predis/predis": "~1.0"
    }
}
```

Then run Composer:

```
$ composer update
```

In this section, the PHP code has comments that represent the result of the previous expression. It is recommended to run all of the code from this section in an interactive PHP interpreter (PsySH is recommended: http://psysh.org/).

The basic commands in PHP

Predis is a full-feature client, and most of Redis's commands can be accessed through a very simple interface. Each executed command returns a value synchronously. Some basic commands are shown in the following lines, and after this, you should be able to figure out how most of them work:

```
require 'vendor/autoload.php';
Predis\Autoloader::register();
$client = new Predis\Client(array('host' => '127.0.0.1',
'port' => 6379), array('prefix' =>'php:'));

$client->set("string:my_key", "Hello World");
$client->get("string:my_key");
# "Hello World"
$client->incr("string:counter");
$client->mget(array("string:my_key", "string:counter"));
# array('Hello World', '2')
```

```php
$client->rpush("list:my_list", "item1", "item2");
$client->lpop("list:my_list");
# 'item1'

$client->hset("set:redis_book", "title", "Redis Essentials");
$client->hgetall("set:redis_book");
# array('title' => 'Redis Essentials')

$client->sadd("set:users", "alice", "bob");
$client->smembers("set:users");
# array('bob', 'alice')

$client->zadd("sorted_set:programmers", 1940, "Alan Kay");
$client->zadd("sorted_set:programmers", 1912, "Alan Turing");
$client->zrange("sorted_set:programmers", 0, -1, "withscores");
# array('Alan Turing' => 1912, 'Alan Kay' => 1940)
```

The blocking commands in PHP

There are three List commands that are connection-blocking: **BRPOP**, **BLPOP**, and **BRPOPLPUSH**. In the Node.js client that we presented, these commands expect a callback, but in Predis, they don't expect callbacks. They return values, and no call is deferred.

The **BRPOP** and **BLPOP** commands expect a list of keys and a timeout. **BRPOPLPUSH** expects a source key, a destination key, and a timeout. The timeout parameter in all the three commands is optional and defaults to zero. If the timeout is zero, the call will hang until an item is found in any of the specified source keys. These commands are called blocking commands because the Redis client is blocked until there is at least one element in the List or until the timeout has been exceeded:

- **BRPOP**: This is the blocking version of **RPOP**. An element is popped from the tail of the first List that is nonempty, with the given keys being checked in the order in which they were given

- **BLPOP**: This is the blocking version of **LPOP**. An element is popped from the head of the first List that is nonempty, with the given keys being checked in the order in which they were given

- **BRPOPLPUSH**: An element is popped from the tail of the source key and inserted at the head of the destination key

The preceding commands are shown in the following code:

```
require 'vendor/autoload.php';
Predis\Autoloader::register();
$client = new Predis\Client(array('host' => '127.0.0.1',
                                  'port' => 6379),
                            array('prefix' => 'php:'));

$client->lpush('blocking:queue', 'first');
$client->lpush('blocking:queue', 'second');

$client->blpop(['blocking:queue'], 0);
# array('php:blocking:queue', 'second')

$client->brpop(['blocking:queue'], 0);
# array('php:blocking:queue', 'first')

$client->rpush('blocking:source', 'message');
$client->brpoplpush('blocking:source', 'blocking:destination', 0);
# 'message'
```

Pipelines in PHP

Predis provides two ways to work with pipelines:

- A client can return a pipeline instance with a fluent interface, providing the ability to chain commands
- A client can execute a pipeline inside an anonymous function (this is very similar to callbacks in Node.js, but in Predis, it is not asynchronous)

The following code shows how to use pipelines:

```
require 'vendor/autoload.php';
Predis\Autoloader::register();
$client = new Predis\Client(array('host' => '127.0.0.1',
                                  'port' => 6379),
                            array('prefix' => 'php:'));

# fluent interface
$client->pipeline()
        ->sadd("cards:suits", 'hearts')
        ->sadd("cards:suits", 'spades')
        ->sadd("cards:suits", 'diamonds')
        ->sadd("cards:suits", 'clubs')
```

```
        ->smembers("cards:suits")
        ->execute();
# array(1,1,1,1, array('diamonds', 'hearts', 'clubs', 'spades'))


# anonymous function
$client->pipeline(function ($pipe) {
    $pipe->scard("cards:suits");
    $pipe->smembers("cards:suits");
});
# array(4, array('diamonds', 'hearts', 'clubs', 'spades'))
```

The preceding code creates a pipeline, then adds some elements through **SADD**, and then invokes **SMEMBERS** on that Set. The pipeline is sent to Redis when *pipeline.execute()* is called, and the resultant value is an array with one value for each operation called on that pipeline object.

The second pipeline is created using an anonymous function that has a pipeline instance as the argument (*$pipe*), and this argument is used to execute the Redis commands in an isolated context. Even though a function is passed in, the call is still synchronous.

Transactions in PHP

Predis provides an abstraction for Redis transactions based on **MULTI** and **EXEC** with an interface that is very similar to pipelines.

A client returns a transaction instance with a fluent interface, providing the ability to chain commands:

```
require 'vendor/autoload.php';
Predis\Autoloader::register();
$client = new Predis\Client(array('host' => '127.0.0.1',
                                  'port' => 6379),
                            array('prefix' => 'php:'));


$client->transaction()
       ->set('transaction:key',
             'A string in a transactional block')
       ->incr( 'transaction:counter')
       ->get('transaction:key')
       ->execute();
# array("Predis\Response\Status => OK", 2,
        "A string in a transactional block")
```

Scripting in PHP

Predis has an interesting approach to scripting: it provides a higher level abstraction to register commands and access them as if they were native Redis commands.

Internally, Predis uses the command **EVALSHA**, but **EVAL** is used as a fallback if needed. It is necessary to create a PHP class that extends *Predis\Command\ScriptCommand* and implements two methods: *getKeysCount* and *getScript*:

- *getKeysCount*: This returns the number of arguments that should be considered as keys
- *getScript*: This returns the body of a Lua code

A class called *MultiplyValue* is defined in the following code, which is an abstraction used to create a multiply command.

This command will obtain the value of a key, multiply it by the number specified as the argument, and update the key with the new value:

```php
require 'vendor/autoload.php';
Predis\Autoloader::register();
$client = new Predis\Client(array('host' => '127.0.0.1',
                                  'port' => 6379),
                            array('prefix' => 'php:'));

class MultiplyValue extends Predis\Command\ScriptCommand {
  public function getKeysCount() {
    return 1;
  }

  public function getScript() {
    $lua = <<<LUASCRIPT
      local value = redis.call('GET', KEYS[1])
      value = tonumber(value)
      local newvalue = value * ARGV[1]
      redis.call('SET', KEYS[1], newvalue)
      return newvalue
    LUASCRIPT;
    return $lua;
  }
}

$client->getProfile()->defineCommand('multiply', 'MultiplyValue');
$client->set("mynumber", 4);
$client->multiply("mynumber", 2);
# 8
```

The method *defineCommand* needs to be executed to register the new command, **multiply**, in the Predis server profile. The command **multiply** receives two arguments:

- *keyname*: This is a string that represents an existing key. This key should be a string with a number as its value so that the multiplication can be performed

- *factor*: This is the multiplication factor for the key value

 We recommend that you check out the Predis repository and documentation at `https://github.com/nrk/predis`, where you can find many examples and a fully detailed explanation of its commands.

Python

There are many Redis client libraries for the Python language, and we are going to present **redis-py**, the most mature Redis client implementation for Python. The Python version used for all examples is 2.7.

Installing **redis-py** (it is recommended to install it in a virtualenv):

```
$ pip install redis
```

In this section, the Python code has comments that represent the result of the previous expression. It is recommended to run all of the code from this section in the interactive Python interpreter (**python** or **ipython** in the command line).

The basic commands in Python

Most Redis commands are accessed in **redis-py** through a very simple interface. Each executed command returns a value synchronously. Some basic commands are shown in the following code, and after this, you should be able to figure out how most of them work:

```python
import redis
client = redis.StrictRedis(host='localhost', port=6379)

client.set("string:my_key", "Hello World")
client.get("string:my_key")
# "Hello World"
client.incr("string:counter")
client.mget(["string:my_key", "string:counter"])
# ['Hello World', '2']

client.rpush("list:my_list", "item1", "item2")
client.lpop("list:my_list")
```

```
# 'item1'

client.hset("set:redis_book", "title", "Redis Essentials")
client.hgetall("set:redis_book")
# {'title': 'Redis Essentials'}

client.sadd("set:users", "alice", "bob")
client.smembers("set:users")
# set(['bob', 'alice'])

client.zadd("sorted_set:programmers", 1940, "Alan Kay")
client.zadd("sorted_set:programmers", 1912, "Alan Turing")
client.zrange("sorted_set:programmers", 0, -1, withscores=True)
# [('Alan Turing', 1912.0), ('Alan Kay', 1940.0)]
```

As you can see, most of Redis's commands have a pretty straightforward interface, they always return a value, and there are no callbacks involved.

The blocking commands in Python

There are three List commands that are connection-blocking: **BRPOP**, **BLPOP**, and **BRPOPLPUSH**. In **redis-py**, these commands have the same behavior and API as in the previous example in the PHP section:

```
import redis
client = redis.StrictRedis(host='localhost', port=6379)

client.lpush('blocking:queue', 'first')
client.lpush('blocking:queue', 'second')

client.blpop(['blocking:queue'], 0)
# ('blocking:queue', 'first')

client.brpop(['blocking:queue'], 0)
# ('blocking:queue', 'second')

client.rpush('blocking:source', 'message')
client.brpoplpush('blocking:source', 'blocking:destination', 0)
# 'message'
```

Pipelines in Python

Pipelines can be created through a regular function call or a context manager.

By default, pipelines in **redis-py** are wrapped in a transaction — if a transaction is not the desired behavior, the *transaction* parameter needs to be set to *False*:

```
import redis
client = redis.StrictRedis(host='localhost', port=6379)

pipeline = client.pipeline(transaction=False)
pipeline.sadd("cards:suit", "hearts")
pipeline.sadd("cards:suit", "spades")
pipeline.sadd("cards:suit", "diamonds")
pipeline.sadd("cards:suit", "clubs")
pipeline.smembers("cards:suit")
result = pipeline.execute()
# [0, 0, 0, 0, set(['hearts', 'clubs', 'spades', 'diamonds'])]

with client.pipeline() as pipe:
    pipe.scard("cards:suit")
    result = pipe.execute()
    # [4]
```

The preceding code creates the first pipeline without being wrapped in a transaction (it sets the *transaction* parameter to *False*), then adds some elements through the command **SADD**, and then invokes **SMEMBERS** on that set. This pipeline is sent to Redis when *pipeline.execute()* is executed, and the result value is an array with one value for each operation called on that pipeline object.

The second pipeline is created as a context manager (using the *with* keyword), and its interface is the same as the previous *pipeline* object. Because the command **SCARD** is the only command sent to the pipeline, its value is retrieved through the first element of *pipeline.execute()*. The *transaction* parameter has not been changed, and its default value is *True*.

Transactions in Python

There is no exclusive interface for transactions in **redis-py**. Instead, it provides transactional pipelines. The *pipeline()* method needs to be executed with the *transaction* parameter set to *True* to create a transaction.

Although transactional pipelines can be used as a regular object, visually it makes more sense to use them as context managers—the indentation helps in seeing what will be executed as a transaction:

```
import redis
client = redis.StrictRedis(host='localhost', port=6379)

with client.pipeline(transaction=True) as transaction:
    transaction.set('transaction:key',
      'A string in a transactional block')
    transaction.incr('transaction:counter')
    transaction.get('transaction:key')
    result = transaction.execute()
    # [True, 2, 'A string in a transactional block']
```

Scripting in Python

Lua scripting in **redis-py** can be used through three different interfaces: *eval()*, *evalsha()*, and a *Script* object created by *register_script()*.

The following snippet shows how to use a Lua script to multiply a Redis key by a number and save the result in the key.

The first interface shown is the *eval()* function, which receives the following as arguments:

- The Lua script as a string
- The number of keys that are going to be passed
- The Redis keys that the script is going to use (the *KEYS* variable inside the script)
- The values that the script is going to use (the *ARGV* variable inside the script)

The return value is the result of the Lua script evaluated:

```
import redis
client = redis.StrictRedis(host='localhost', port=6379)

lua_script = """
    local value = redis.call('GET', KEYS[1])
    value = tonumber(value)
    local newvalue = value * ARGV[1]
    redis.call('SET', KEYS[1], newvalue)
    return newvalue
""" # 1
```

```
client.set('python:value', 30)
client.eval(lua_script, 1, "python:value", 3)
# "90"
```

The second interface is the *load_script()* and *evalsha()* functions. The *load_script()* function receives as an argument the Lua script (as a string) and returns its SHA value (this is the same thing as running the Redis command **LOAD SCRIPT**).

The *evalsha()* function receives the following as arguments:

- The SHA value of a script
- The number of keys that are going to be passed into the script
- The Redis keys available inside the script (the *KEYS* variable inside the script)
- The values available in the script (the *ARGV* variable inside the script)

This function returns the result of the Lua script:

```
client.set('python:value', 30)
sha = client.script_load(lua_script)
client.evalsha(sha, 1, 'python:value', 3)
# "90"
```

The last interface, *register_script()*, receives as an argument a Lua script as string and it returns a *Script* instance. In the preceding example, the script was assigned to the variable *multiply*.

The *multiply* object (a *Script* instance) is callable, and it receives as arguments the values of *KEYS* and *ARGV*, which are going to be available inside the Lua script. This interface is the recommended way of interacting with Lua scripts because it transforms the script into a Python object that behaves like a regular Python function:

```
client.set('python:value', 30)
multiply = client.register_script(lua_script)
multiply(keys=['python:value'], args=[3])

# "90"
```

The official documentation of **redis-py** can be found at https://redis-py. readthedocs.org, and its GitHub repository is at https://github.com/ andymccurdy/redis-py.

Ruby

Redis has an official Ruby client, **redis-rb**, and this is the client used in this section.

Installing it:

```
$ gem install redis
```

In this section, the Ruby code has comments that represent the result of the previous expression. It is recommended to run all of the code from this section in the interactive Ruby interpreter (**irb** in the command line).

The basic commands in Ruby

The interface of **redis-rb** is very close to how you interact with Redis through **redis-cli**:

```ruby
require 'redis'
@redis = Redis.new(:host => "127.0.0.1", :port => 6379)

@redis.set "string:my_key", "Hello World"
@redis.get "string:my_key"
# => "Hello World"
@redis.incr "string:counter"
@redis.mget ["string:my_key", "string:counter"]
# => ["Hello World", "1"]

@redis.rpush "list:my_list", ["item1", "item2"]
@redis.lpop "list:my_list"
# => "item1"

@redis.hset "set:redis_book", "title", "Redis Essentials"
@redis.hgetall "set:redis_book"
# => {"title"=>"Redis Essentials"}

@redis.sadd "set:users", ["alice", "bob"]
@redis.smembers "set:users"
# => ["bob", "alice"]

@redis.zadd "sorted_set:programmers", 1940, "Alan Kay"
@redis.zadd "sorted_set:programmers", 1912, "Alan Turing"
@redis.zrange "sorted_set:programmers", 0, -1, :withscores => true

# => [["Alan Turing", 1912.0], ["Alan Kay", 1940.0]]
```

The blocking commands in Ruby

The behavior and API of the blocking commands in **redis-rb** are the same as in the previous PHP and Python implementations:

```ruby
require 'redis'
@redis = Redis.new(:host => "127.0.0.1", :port => 6379)

@redis.rpush 'blocking:queue', 'first'
@redis.rpush 'blocking:queue', 'second'

@redis.blpop ['blocking:queue'], 0
# => ["blocking:queue", "first"]

@redis.brpop ['blocking:queue'], 0
# => ["blocking:queue", "second"]

@redis.lpush 'blocking:source', 'message'
@redis.brpoplpush 'blocking:source', 'blocking:destination', 0
# => "message"
```

Pipelines in Ruby

In **redis-rb**, pipelines are created through the method *Redis#pipelined*, and it expects a block to run the commands inside the pipeline:

```ruby
require 'redis'
@redis = Redis.new(:host => "127.0.0.1", :port => 6379)

result = @redis.pipelined do
  @redis.sadd "cards:suits", "hearts"
  @redis.sadd "cards:suits", "spades"
  @redis.sadd "cards:suits", "diamonds"
  @redis.sadd "cards:suits", "clubs"
  @redis.smembers "cards:suits"
end
# => [false, false, false, false, ["diamonds", "spades", "clubs",
"hearts"]]
```

The *Redis#pipelined* block does not expect parameters, and all Redis commands are called on the Redis client object (in the preceding case, it is *@redis*). The result of the *Redis#pipelined* call is an array with a value for each command executed inside the block.

All replies from individual commands that are executed in a pipeline can be accessed through a *Future* object. When the pipeline has successfully completed, the value of that *Future* object becomes available. Here is an example of this:

```
require 'redis'
@redis = Redis.new(:host => "127.0.0.1", :port => 6379)

@redis.pipelined do
  @redis.set "message", "hello world"
  @message = @redis.get "message"
end

@message.value
# => "hello world"
```

Transactions in Ruby

A transaction is created in **redis-rb** through the *Redis#multi* method, which expects a block with a parameter, and all the commands to be executed in a transaction are executed on that block parameter. Transactions in Redis are executed through **MULTI/EXEC**, but in **redis-rb**, the **EXEC** command is not sent. It is implicitly called after *Redis#multi* is called:

```
@redis.multi do |multi|
  multi.set "transaction:key", "A string in a transactional block"
  multi.incr "transaction:counter"
end

@redis.get "transaction:key"
# => "A string in a transactional block"
```

Scripting in Ruby

There are two ways of using scripts in **redis-rb**: *Redis#eval* and *Redis#evalsha*. These have the same interface as their equivalent Redis commands: the former expects a Lua script and immediately executes it; the latter executes a cached Lua script identified by its SHA value.

The following snippet shows how to use both *Redis#eval* and *Redis#evalsha* through a Lua script that multiplies a key by a number and modifies the key that has the result as its value:

```
lua_script = <<EOS
    local value = redis.call('GET', KEYS[1])
```

```
      value = tonumber(value)
      local newvalue = value * ARGV[1]
      redis.call('SET', KEYS[1], newvalue)
      return newvalue
EOS

@redis.set "script:my_value", 30
@redis.eval(lua_script, {
  :keys => ["script:my_value"],
  :argv => [3]
})
# => "90"


@redis.set "script:my_value", 30
multiply_script_sha = @redis.script :load, lua_script
@redis.evalsha(multiply_script_sha, {
  :keys => ["script:my_value"],
  :argv => [3]
})
# => "90"
```

The official Git repository of **redis-rb** is `https://github.com/redis/redis-rb`, and it has a good set of examples and a brief documentation can be found in the *README.md* file.

Summary

In this chapter, you learned how PHP, Ruby, and Python clients work. You also learned how to execute basic commands, create scripts, and work with blocking commands, pipelines, and transactions.

The next chapter is going to show you the common pitfalls when working with Redis, such as using the wrong data type for a problem, using multiple databases, using the swap space, and not planning the memory properly.

6
Common Pitfalls (Avoiding Traps)

In this chapter, we will describe some common pitfalls when using Redis, including keys without a namespace, using an inappropriate data type to solve a problem, and commands that should not be executed in production. Some of these examples are based on previous experience at Yipit (www.yipit.com) as well as other companies.

The wrong data type for the job

When we learn about a new feature of a tool, we often unconsciously try to apply it to our current set of problems. Many times, there is nothing wrong with this, but that's not always the case with Redis.

At Yipit, we used to store all deals that were going to be sent to users in a Redis Set. Although the solution worked, developers thought it was memory-inefficient because the Yipit user base was large. To rectify this issue, some of the developers thought that changing the Set implementation to a Bitmap implementation would make the solution memory-efficient. In other contexts, Bitmaps performed so well that developers thought they were the answer to everything—this turned out to be untrue.

No benchmark tests were performed based on the wrong assumption that Bitmaps would always be more memory-efficient than Sets.

The Bitmap implementation sounded logical and was deployed to production. The DevOps engineers received alerts and noticed that the Redis memory was full. The next sections describe the architecture and show how the memory problems could have been prevented.

> We strongly recommend the use of benchmarks before committing to a solution.

The Set approach

The Set implementation was very straightforward: each user was represented by a Set, and each Set element was a deal to be sent. The deal IDs were sequential numbers (1, 2, 3, 4, 5, and so on).

The following code is a benchmark of this implementation, using 100,000 Sets with 12 deal IDs each, and each user will receive the same 12 deals.

Create a file called *benchmark-set.js* in the *chapter 6* folder with the following code:

```
var redis = require("redis");
var client = redis.createClient();
var MAX_USERS = 100000;
var MAX_DEALS = 12;
var MAX_DEAL_ID = 10000;

for (var i = 0 ; i < MAX_USERS ; i++) {
  var multi = client.multi();
  for (var j = 0 ; j < MAX_DEALS ; j++) {
    multi.sadd("set:user:" + i, MAX_DEAL_ID - j, 1);
  }
  multi.exec();
}

client.quit();
```

Remove all of the existing data from Redis, execute the benchmark, and then retrieve the used memory (this may take a couple of minutes):

```
$ redis-cli FLUSHALL && node benchmark-set.js && redis-cli INFO memory
OK
# Memory
used_memory:14860000
used_memory_human:14.17M
used_memory_rss:147779584
used_memory_peak:2542119984
used_memory_peak_human:2.37G
```

```
used_memory_lua:35840
mem_fragmentation_ratio:9.94
mem_allocator:libc
```

The benchmark output may vary across computers, but it is enough to compare the cost magnitudes of the Set and Bitmap implementations.

The Bitmap approach

In the Bitmap implementation, each user is identified by a Bitmap. Each Bitmap will have the deals that are going to be sent by being marked as 1, and all other deals will be marked as 0.

Unlike the Set implementation, the Bitmap cost is based on the highest deal ID present. If the highest deal ID is 10, the Bitmap is going to cost 11 bits (the zero is included); if the highest deal ID is 1,000,000, the Bitmap is going to cost 1,000,001 bits.

To refresh your knowledge of Bitmaps, reread *chapter 2, Advanced Data Types (Earning a Black Belt)*.

The following code is a benchmark of the Bitmap implementation, using 100,000 Bitmaps with 12 deals each, and each user will receive the same 12 deals. Bitmaps with the highest 12 deal IDs are the worst scenario.

Create a file called *benchmark-bitmap.js* in the *chapter 6* folder with the following code:

```
var redis = require("redis");
var client = redis.createClient();
var MAX_USERS = 100000;
var MAX_DEALS = 12;
var MAX_DEAL_ID = 10000;

for (var i = 0 ; i < MAX_USERS ; i++) {
  var multi = client.multi();
  for (var j = 0 ; j < MAX_DEALS ; j++) {
    multi.setbit("bitmap:user:" + i, MAX_DEAL_ID - j, 1);
  }
  multi.exec();
}

client.quit();
```

Remove all of the existing data from Redis, execute the benchmark, and then retrieve the used memory (this may take a couple of minutes):

```
$ redis-cli FLUSHALL && node benchmark-bitmap.js && redis-cli INFO memory
OK
# Memory
used_memory:266060416
used_memory_human:253.73M
used_memory_rss:337969152
used_memory_peak:2542119984
used_memory_peak_human:2.37G
used_memory_lua:35840
mem_fragmentation_ratio:1.27
mem_allocator:libc
```

The Bitmap implementation used approximately 253 MB while the Set implementation used approximately 14 MB. The Bitmap implementation (which was supposed to be cheaper) costs 18 times more in the scenario described earlier.

Multiple Redis databases

Redis comes with support for multiple databases, which is very similar to the concept in SQL databases. In SQL databases, such as MySQL, PostgreSQL, and Oracle, you can define a name for your databases. However, Redis databases are represented by numbers.

You learned in *Chapter 4, Commands (Where the Wild Things Are)*, that we can switch between databases using the command **SELECT <dbid>**. Although multiple databases work fine, this has become a deprecated feature, so we do not recommend that you use it in production.

It has been deprecated because it is, in general, better to launch multiple Redis servers on the same machine rather than using multiple databases. Redis is single threaded. Thus, a single Redis server with multiple databases only uses one CPU core. On the other hand, if multiple Redis servers are used, it is possible to take advantage of multiple CPU cores.

Multiple databases make administration of Redis harder and may complicate performance and resource usage diagnosis. It would not be easy to figure out which database is causing issues.

Some Redis clients do not even support multiple Redis databases, since it would make it hard to create a thread-safe implementation.

Keys without a namespace

It is good practice to use namespaces when defining your keys in Redis in order to avoid key name collisions and to organize your keys based on your application section or area.

In SQL databases, a namespace can be represented by the database name or the database tables.

Also, in a SQL database, it is reasonable to assume that a database called `music-online` has tables called `album`, `song`, and `author`.

Redis does not support namespacing. Usually, key name conventions are used to mimic namespaces. A common way of adding namespaces to Redis keys is by prepending a namespace (that is, **namespace:key_name**). Some Redis clients support addition of a prefix to all Redis keys.

Here are a few examples of key names with namespaces:

- *music-online:song:1*
- *music-online:song:2*
- *music-online:album:10001:metadata*
- *music-online:album:10001:songs*
- *music-online:author:123*

 Multiple databases are not an excuse not to use proper key naming. Always use consistent namespaces.

Using Swap

There is a Linux kernel parameter called **swappiness** that controls when the operating system will start using the swap space. This parameter can be set to values between 0 and 100. A lower value tells the kernel to use the swap space less frequently, and a higher value tells it to use the swap space more frequently. The default value is 60.

Here are some special cases of using swaps:

Value	Strategy
vm.swappiness = 0	• Linux 3.5 and newer: Disables swap entirely • Linux 3.4 and older: Swap only to avoid an "out of memory" condition
vm.swappiness = 1	• Linux 3.5 and newer: Minimum amount of swapping without disabling it entirely
vm.swappiness = 100	• Linux will swap aggressively

In a scenario where Redis needs to access from the swap space, the OS needs to move the necessary pages back into the RAM. During this process, Redis is blocked until the OS finishes its job.

We recommend that you use a swappiness of 0 when your data always fits into the RAM and 1 when you are not sure.

To disable swap usage in Linux 3.5 and newer, execute the following as the root user:

```
sysctl -w vm.swappiness=0
```

To make the previous change permanent across reboots, change the file */etc/sysctl.conf* (as the root user) to include the following:

```
vm.swappiness=0
```

Not planning and configuring the memory properly

The Redis server needs enough memory to perform backups if any strategy is enabled. In the worst-case scenario, **redis-server** may double the used memory during the backup.

During RDB snapshot creation and AOF rewriting, **redis-server** needs to duplicate itself (it executes the *fork()* system call). *Chapter 8, Scaling Redis (Beyond a Single Instance)*, will introduce AOF and RDB, with details.

If the Redis instance is very busy during the *fork()* call, it is possible that the copy-on-write strategy and overcommitting the memory is not enough. In this case, the child process may need the same amount of memory (or an amount very close to it) as the parent.

Assuming that Linux is the operating system, set the overcommit memory configuration to 1 to boost background saves. Add the following to the */etc/sysctl.conf* file:

```
vm.overcommit_memory=1
```

After saving */etc/sysctl.conf*, reboot the server.

There is a configuration directive called **maxmemory** that limits the amount of memory that Redis is allowed to use (in bytes). Change this configuration to the appropriate value based on the available memory and application requirements.

Redis should not use more than 50 percent of the available memory when any backup strategy is enabled. Make sure that you set up alarms for Redis memory usage.

An inappropriate persistence strategy

Once at Yipit, a Redis instance (read-intensive) was experiencing some slowdowns, but nobody could understand why. At first, the DevOps team thought that the application's code was making Redis slow, but after some investigation, they found that the issue was due to a periodic backup strategy. *Chapter 8, Scaling Redis (Beyond a Single Instance)*, will cover persistence in depth.

When Redis starts the procedure to create an RDB snapshot or rewrite the AOF file, it creates a child process (using the *fork()* system call), and the new process handles the procedure.

During the *fork()* execution, the process is blocked and Redis will stop serving clients. This is when the perceived latency by clients increases.

The Yipit problem was due to a long *fork()* time on AWS. The instance type family used was **M2**, which is a family of **ParaVirtual** (**PV**) machines, as opposed to **Hardware-assisted Virtual Machines** (**HVM**). It is known that the *fork()* system call in a PV machine is slower than in an HVM machine. This is a great example of low-level behavior that you cannot change and may find difficult to control.

Here are some ideas of what to do in such a case:

- Disable the transparent huge pages Linux kernel feature
  (echo never > /sys/kernel/mm/transparent_hugepage/enabled)
- Use an HVM instance
- Use a persistence-only slave server, in which the slave does nothing but cause the replicated data to persist

- Make backups less frequent, if possible, and then check whether the problem is mitigated

- Disable automatic persistence in Redis. Make the data persist manually when Redis is not under heavy load (with a *cron* job or something similar)

- Disable persistence if the data can be recreated easily and quickly

Redislab has a detailed benchmark of fork time on AWS/Xen at `https://redislabs.com/blog/testing-fork-time-on-awsxen-infrastructure`.

Summary

This chapter presented common Redis pitfalls such as using the wrong data type, using multiple Redis databases, and not using namespaces for key names. It also told you how to avoid them. Then it showed the pitfalls of the swap space, not planning the memory properly, and using an inappropriate persistence strategy.

The next chapter will discuss some security techniques, such as authentication, firewall configuration, and SSL encryption.

7
Security Techniques (Guard Your Data)

Redis was designed to be used in a trusted private network. It supports a very basic security system to protect the connection between the client and server via a plain-text password.

It is important to protect the Redis instances. An attack on an unprotected instance could put your data into unauthorized hands. Also, the command **FLUSHALL** can be used by an external attacker, which could cause you to lose all of your data.

We will explain some techniques of using the existing security mechanisms in Redis as well as other approaches to improving security around Redis.

The basic security

When Redis was designed, the main goals were maximum performance and simplicity, rather than maximum security. Although Redis implements a basic security mechanism, which is based on plain-text passwords, Redis does not implement **Access Control List (ACL)**. Therefore, it is not possible to have users with different permission levels.

The authentication feature can be enabled through the configuration **requirepass**. Since Redis is superfast, requirepass could be dangerous as a malicious user could potentially guess thousands of passwords in a second. Avoid this by choosing a complex password of at least 64 characters.

After it is enabled, Redis will reject any commands from unauthenticated clients.

Copy the default *redis.conf* file to the *chapter 7* folder, which is in the Redis source code directory. Every time the Redis configuration file is changed, the **redis-server** needs to be restarted; otherwise, the changes will not be applied.

Add the following to *redis.conf*:

```
requirepass a7f$f35eceb7e@3edd502D892f5885007869dd2f80434Fed5b4!fac00
57f51fM
```

Restart the **redis-server** by specifying *redis.conf* (repeat this step after every configuration change):

```
$ redis-server /path/to/chapter7/redis.conf
```

The command **AUTH** authenticates a Redis client, as mentioned in *Chapter 4, Commands (Where the Wild Things Are)*:

```
$ redis-cli
127.0.0.1:6379> SET hello world
(error) NOAUTH Authentication required.
127.0.0.1:6379> AUTH a7f$f35eceb7e@3edd502D892f5885007869dd2f80434Fed5b4!
fac0057f51fM
OK
127.0.0.1:6379> SET hello world
OK
```

The **redis-server** will return an OK status if the password used in the command **AUTH** matches the password in the *redis.conf* file. From that point onward, the server will accept any commands from that client.

An error stating that the password is invalid will be returned if the password is wrong, and the client will have to try again with a new password.

It is important to know that the **AUTH** command is similar to every other command in Redis. It is sent unencrypted, which means that it is not protected against any attacker who has enough access to the network to perform eavesdropping.

Obfuscating critical commands

Another interesting technique is obfuscating or disabling some critical commands, such as **FLUSHDB**, **FLUSHALL**, **CONFIG**, **KEYS**, **DEBUG**, and **SAVE**. To disable a command, you should set the new name to an empty string.

Some applications might still need some of these critical commands available in production. In such cases, we recommend that you rename them to avoid accidental calls from external clients. The new names should be hard to guess. The new command names are still available but obfuscated.

Renaming a command does not ensure security, because a malicious attacker can still use brute force to find the command name.

It is good practice to create a configuration file called *rename-commands.conf* for organization purposes. Use the directive *include* in *redis.conf* to include the *rename-commands.conf* file.

Create a file called *renamed-commands.conf* in the *chapter 7* folder with the following code:

```
rename-command FLUSHDB e0cc96ad2eab73c2c347011806a76b73
rename-command FLUSHALL a31907b21c437f46808ea49322c91d23a
rename-command CONFIG ""
rename-command KEYS ""
rename-command DEBUG ""
rename-command SAVE ""
```

Let's look at each of these commands in detail:

- **FLUSHDB/FLUSHALL**: These commands are very critical. Since they delete all of your data in Redis, you should disable/rename them.

- **CONFIG**: Ideally, you would disable/rename the command **CONFIG** in production, because it gives access to all the options set in your **redis.conf** file to the client.

- **KEYS**: This command will block Redis while it is executing, and since this command runs in linear time over all existing keys, it is recommended that you disable/rename it.

- **DEBUG**: This command can force a crash in the **redis-server (DEBUG SEGFAULT)**, and you should disable/rename it.

- **SAVE**: This command should be disabled in production since it will block all other clients during the process of saving the data in a file. Also, we recommend that you use **BGSAVE** instead.

Add the following to *redis.conf* and then restart the **redis-server**:

```
include /path/to/chapter7/rename-commands.conf
```

Redis returns an unknown command error when a disabled/renamed command is executed with its original name:

```
$ redis-cli
127.0.0.1:6379> SAVE
(error) ERR unknown command 'SAVE'
```

```
127.0.0.1:6379> FLUSHALL
(error) ERR unknown command 'FLUSHALL'
127.0.0.1:6379> a31907b21c437f46808ea49322c91d23a
OK
```

 Keep in mind that renaming commands that are transmitted to slaves can cause problems.

Networking security

Redis is meant to run in a trusted network, but that is not always the case. Currently, many Redis servers are deployed on public clouds, meaning security is a concern.

There are many ways to make Redis secure, such as the following:

- Use firewall rules to block access from unknown clients
- Run Redis on the loopback interface, rather than a publicly accessible network interface
- Run Redis in a virtual private cloud instead of the public Internet
- Encrypt client-to-server communication

Protecting Redis with firewall rules

Firewall rules are a safe alternative to protect a Redis server, but it is required to have a list of all the trusted **Classless Inter-Domain Routing (CIDR)** blocks of the possible clients. In a Unix-like server, the **iptables** program can be used to set up firewall rules.

The **iptables** program is a standard firewall created in 1998 by Rusty Russell. It is included in most Linux distributions by default. Most of the explanation of **iptables** is not applicable for Windows or Mac OS. However, because Redis will be running on a Linux server most of the time, it is important to understand how **iptables** can be used to improve the security around Redis. The **iptables** program should be executed by the root user.

In summary, **iptables** defines the rules to govern the network traffic. The **iptables** program performs packet filtering with network rules. The idea is as follows: different tables have multiple chains, and a chain is a group of rules that a packet is checked against sequentially. When a packet matches one of the existing rules in **iptables**, it will execute the associated action. The default table is the "filter" table.

There are three built-in chains for the filter table:

- **INPUT**: This chain handles all packets that are addressed to your server
- **OUTPUT**: This chain contains the rules for the traffic created by your server
- **FORWARD**: This chain allows you to configure your server to route requests to other machines

In this section, some **iptables** snippets are presented. They will configure **iptables** to accept or deny connections from some IPs.

Allow all IPs in the address space of *192.16.1* to connect to the server:

```
iptables -A INPUT -s 192.168.1.0/24 -j ACCEPT
```

Allow only the individual IP *10.10.48.34* to connect to the server:

```
iptables -A INPUT -s 10.10.48.34 -j ACCEPT
```

Set the default policy for all **INPUT** chains to drop all packets:

```
iptables -P INPUT DROP
```

Set the default policy for all **FORWARD** chains to drop all packets:

```
iptables -P FORWARD DROP
```

> Modifications to the **iptables** rules are saved in memory, and they live until the next reboot or until **iptables** is restarted. To cause the modifications to persist, execute the program **iptables-save**.
>
> **iptables** is a very powerful tool, and we recommend that you learn more about it. The successor of **iptables** is called **nftables**, and we also recommend that you read about it.

When Redis is running on the cloud, you may need to check your cloud provider's documentation to learn how to set up firewall rules on your Redis server.

In a scenario where **Amazon Web Services (AWS)** is the cloud provider, check their documentation on how to set up security groups, that is, how AWS configures firewall rules for their instances.

With AWS, you can create firewall rules based on CIDR blocks and security group IDs (all firewall configurations are saved in security groups) as shown in the following screenshot:

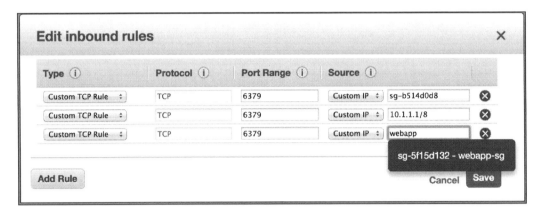

 It is more flexible to create firewall rules based on security group IDs than on CIDR blocks.

Running Redis on the loopback network interface

In a scenario where a web application and the **redis-server** are running on the same machine, you should bind **redis-server** to the loopback interface (*127.0.0.1*). This approach blocks external access to Redis, and the loopback interface is faster than a physical network interface (the loopback interface is a virtual interface that never changes its address).

You can bind **redis-server** to the loopback interface by changing *redis.conf* to have the following:

```
bind 127.0.0.1
```

After making this change, restart the **redis-server**.

Running Redis in a Virtual Private Cloud

Currently, a few public cloud providers offer **Virtual Private Clouds (VPCs)**, and VPCs can be very useful for managing Redis servers' security.

A VPC is a pool of on-demand resources that run on a public cloud. The resources are virtually isolated from different users of the same public cloud.

For example, all machines can reach each other in a public cloud if no restrictive firewall rules are defined, but in a VPC, this is not the case. Only machines on the same VPC can reach each other.

VPCs may sound extremely complicated, but cloud providers make them simpler to work with, and it is a great idea to run Redis on a VPC.

It is also a good idea to have firewall rules set up for a Redis server even if it is in a VPC, because you can ensure that Redis is only accessed by trusted services.

Encrypting client-to-server communication

By default, Redis does not support any encryption. Assuming that encryption is desired in the client-server connection, extra tools are necessary. Encrypting the Redis communication using SSL can prevent malicious attackers from eavesdropping on the network, and ensure that only trusted clients that have the SSL key can connect to Redis.

The tool we will use to encrypt Redis communication is called **stunnel**. It is an SSL encryption wrapper between a local client and a local or remote server. Many services that do not implement SSL encryption can take advantage of **stunnel**.

Redis can be combined with **stunnel** to encrypt all client-server communication.

The basic idea is that a connection will exist between a **stunnel** server and a client, and that connection will be SSL-encrypted through a private SSL key.

There are two options for running Redis with **stunnel**:

- Run **stunnel** on both the server and client machines, using the same private key:
    - The **stunnel** in the server creates a tunnel to the **redis-server**

      °   The **stunnel** in the client creates a tunnel to the remote **stunnel** (on the server machine). The Redis client should connect to the local **stunnel**

- Run **stunnel** on the server, and a Redis client that supports SSL must be used. This client will use the private key to encrypt the connection

The following examples require **openssl** and **stunnel** to be installed, and they also require an SSL key.

Go to the *chapter 7* folder and execute the following commands to create the required SSL key:

```
$ openssl genrsa -out key.pem 4096
$ openssl req -new -x509 -key key.pem -out cert.pem -days 1826 -batch
$ cat key.pem cert.pem > private.pem
$ chmod 640 key.pem cert.pem private.pem
```

Running stunnel on both the server and the client

For simplicity, this example will create two configurations that represent the client and the server on the same machine. The server configuration will bind **stunnel** to *0.0.0.0* and port *6666*, and the client configuration will bind **stunnel** to localhost and port *5555*.

In a real-world scenario, these configurations will live on separate machines.

This example will require three terminal windows. The first window will run **stunnel** using the server configuration, the second will run the client configuration, and the third will run the **redis-cli**.

Create the file *stunnel-server.conf* in the *chapter 7* folder with the following content:

```
foreground = yes
cert = private.pem
[redis]
accept = 0.0.0.0:6666
connect = 127.0.0.1:6379
```

This file configures **stunnel** to create an encrypted tunnel between two different network interfaces (*0.0.0.0* and *127.0.0.1*) using *private.pem* as the private key.

Start **stunnel** with the previous server configuration:

```
$ stunnel stunnel-server.conf
```

On the client side, **stunnel** will run slightly differently. Create the file *stunnel-client. conf* in the *chapter 7* folder with the following content:

```
foreground = yes
cert = private.pem
client = yes
[redis]
accept = 127.0.0.1:5555
connect = 0.0.0.0:6666
```

In a different terminal, start another **stunnel** process with the previous client configuration:

```
$ stunnel stunnel-client.conf
```

In another terminal, test the client-server connection with **redis-cli** by running the **PING** command on the client (make sure that you see the PONG reply):

```
$ redis-cli -h 127.0.0.1 -p 5555
127.0.0.1:6379> PING
PONG
```

Running stunnel on the server and using a Redis client that supports SSL

In this scenario, all the previous steps are required to set up the **stunnel** server configuration, but the client configuration is not necessary. Use an SSL-capable Redis client and pass the private key file to it. This approach is preferable because it does not require any additional services or configurations—only the SSL key.

 At the time of writing this book, the client *node_redis* does not support SSL, but a pull request is open for this on GitHub at https://github.com/mranney/node_redis/pull/527.

The next example uses the *redis-py* client, which supports SSL encryption. Create a file called *pythonssl.py* in the *chapter 7* folder with the following code:

```
import redis # 1
import ssl # 2

pool = redis.ConnectionPool(
    connection_class=redis.SSLConnection,
    host='0.0.0.0',
    port=6666,
```

```
        ssl_ca_certs='private.pem',
        ssl_cert_reqs=ssl.CERT_REQUIRED) # 3
r = redis.StrictRedis(connection_pool=pool) # 4

print(r.ping()) # 5
```

1. Import the *redis* client library.

2. Then import the *ssl* library.

3. Create an SSL connection pool to connect to port *6666*, passing the same *private.pem* file that was previously created and is being used by **stunnel**.

4. Create a Redis connection object passing the connection pool.

5. Execute the **PING** command and display `True` if it returned PONG. Otherwise, display `False`.

Then execute it:

```
$ python pythonssl.py
True
```

> Benjamin Cane has written a very good blog post on how to use **stunnel** and Redis, which can be found at `http://bencane.com/2014/02/18/sending-redis-traffic-through-an-ssl-tunnel-with-stunnel/`.

Summary

This chapter presented how to set up basic authentication in Redis and how to obfuscate and disable Redis commands. It also introduced networking techniques to make sure that the Redis connection is safer (firewall, VPC, and SSL encryption). The next chapter will introduce replication, persistence methods (RDB and AOF), data partitioning, and the use of twemproxy to automatically shard data across multiple instances.

8
Scaling Redis (Beyond a Single Instance)

This chapter will show alternative ways to scale Redis horizontally (using multiple instances rather than adding resources to a single instance) using concepts such as persistence, replication, and partitioning. Understanding these concepts is crucial to scale Redis beyond a single instance. By the end of this chapter, you should be able to work with multiple Redis instances and understand the trade-offs of each approach.

Persistence

Since the beginning of this book, we have talked a lot about storing your data in memory using Redis. Memory is transient. Therefore, if a Redis instance is shut down, crashes, or needs to be rebooted, all of the stored data will be lost. To solve this problem, Redis provides two mechanisms to deal with persistence: **Redis Database (RDB)** and **Append-only File (AOF)**. Both of these mechanisms can be used separately or simultaneously in the same Redis instance.

The persistence approach used by Redis has generated a lot of discussion in the community. On March 26, 2012, *Salvatore Sanfilippo* wrote a great blog post demystifying persistence in Redis, since persistence was the most misunderstood feature of Redis.

Recommended reading

Redis persistence demystified at `http://oldblog.antirez.com/post/redis-persistence-demystified.html`.

In this section, we will cover the advantages and disadvantages of each approach as well as how each can be enabled.

RDB (Redis Database)

A *.rdb* file is a binary that has a point in time representing the data stored in a Redis instance. The RDB file format is optimized for fast reads and writes. To achieve the necessary performance, the internal representation of a *.rdb* file on a disk is very similar to Redis's in-memory representation.

Another interesting aspect of RDB is that it can use LZF compression to make an RDB file very compact. LZF compression is a fast compression algorithm that has a very small memory requirement during compression. Although it does not have the best compression rates compared to other compression algorithms, it works efficiently with Redis. Also, a single RDB file is sufficient to restore a Redis instance completely.

RDB is great for backups and disaster recovery because it allows you to save an RDB file every hour, day, week, or month, depending on your needs. This approach allows you to easily use RDB files to restore any dataset at any given time.

The command **SAVE** creates an RDB immediately, but it should be avoided because it blocks the Redis server during snapshot creation. The command **BGSAVE** (background save) should be used instead; it has the same effect as **SAVE**, but it runs in a child process so as not to block Redis.

In order to avoid performance degradation during a background save, the **redis-server** process creates a child process (fork) to perform all the persistence operations. So, the main process will never perform any disk I/O operations. During this process, if the main **redis-server** is receiving writes, the child process will need to copy the memory pages that were changed, and this may increase the total used memory significantly (it uses copy-on-write). Additional information about this can be found in *Chapter 6, Common Pitfalls (Avoiding Traps)*.

The default Redis configuration file, which is in the Redis source code directory, has enabled three snapshot rules to cause the data to persist on the disk through the directive **save**, which performs background saves. This technique is called snapshotting. Open the *redis.conf* file and search for the following three lines:

```
save 900 1
save 300 10
save 60 10000
```

Redis creates snapshots based on two conditions: if in X seconds, Y amount of write operations have happened in your Redis instance, it will create a *.rdb* file. The RDB filename is based on the directive **dbfilename** (this defaults to *dump.rdb*).

The **save** directive's syntax is as follows:

```
save number_of_seconds number_of_changes
```

With this in mind, we can infer what those three lines will do:

1. Save a *.rdb* file on disk every 900 seconds (15 minutes) if at least one write operation happens.

2. Save a *.rdb* file on disk every 300 seconds (5 minutes) if at least 10 write operations happen.

3. Save a *.rdb* file on disk every 60 seconds (1 minute) if at least 10,000 write operations happen.

Having multiple **save** directives provides a lot of flexibility in terms of how often and when snapshots are saved.

With this being said, you can have as many **save** directives as needed in any time interval. However, it is not recommended to use **save** directives less than 30 seconds apart from each other.

Snapshotting can be disabled, which means that nothing will be saved on the disk. This is done by deleting or commenting all **save** directives in the *redis.conf* file and then restarting the Redis server. It can also be disabled via a command-line option or the command **CONFIG SET**.

RDB is not a 100% guaranteed data recovery approach, even if you save snapshots every minute and with at least 100 changes. If the main Redis process stops for any reason, be prepared to lose the latest writes in your database.

Another downside to RDB is that every time that you need to create a snapshot, the Redis main process will execute a *fork()* to create a child process to cause the data to persist on the disk. It can make your Redis instance stop serving clients for milliseconds, sometimes even for a few seconds, depending on the hardware and the size of the dataset. More details about this problem can be found in *Chapter 6, Common Pitfalls (Avoiding Traps)*.

These are the available directives in the Redis configuration for RDB:

- **stop-writes-on-bgsave-error**: The possible values for this are **yes** or **no**. This option makes Redis stop accepting writes if the last background save has failed. Redis starts accepting writes again after a background save succeeds. The default value is **yes**

- **rdbcompression**: The possible values for this are **yes** or **no**. When this option is set to **yes**, Redis uses LZF compression for the *.rdb* files. The default value is **yes**

- **rdbchecksum**: The possible values for this are **yes** or **no**. When it is set to **yes**, Redis saves a checksum at the end of the *.rdb* file and performs a checksum before loading the *.rdb* file. Redis does not start if the RDB checksum does not match with the one in the file. The default value is **yes**

- **dbfilename**: This option sets the *.rdb* filename. The default value is *dump.rdb*

- **save**: This option configures the snapshot frequency, based on the number of seconds and changes. It can be specified multiple times. The default values are *save 3600 1*, *save 300 100*, and *save 60 10000*

- **dir**: This specifies the directory location of the AOF and RDB files

AOF (Append-only File)

When AOF is enabled, every time Redis receives a command that changes the dataset, it will append that command to the AOF (Append-only File). With this being said, if you have AOF enabled and Redis is restarted, it will restore the data by executing all commands listed in AOF, preserving the order, and rebuild the state of the dataset. AOF is an alternative to RDB snapshotting. Until Redis 1.1, Redis only supported the snapshotting strategy, which is not a fully durable approach. Redis 1.1 introduced AOF as a fully durable strategy.

AOF is a "human-readable" append-only log file. This means that there are no seeks and corruption problems can be easily identified. You can even open this file in a text editor and understand what is inside (which is impossible to do with an RDB file, since it is binary). An interesting point to note about AOF is that even in the event of the AOF being incomplete or corrupted for whatever reason, there is a tool called **redis-check-aof** that checks and fixes AOF files easily.

However, this feature comes at the expense of performance and additional disk space.

The AOF can be optimized into a smaller version of itself automatically through a couple of options, or manually through the command **BGREWRITEAOF**. In a crash scenario during the rewrite, the original AOF is not changed.

These are the available directives in the Redis configuration for AOF:

- **appendonly**: This will enable or disable AOF. The options available are **yes** and **no**. By default, AOF is disabled

- **appendfilename:** This specifies the AOF filename. This field is for a filename only, not a file path. It is empty by default

- **appendfsync**: Redis uses a background thread to perform *fsync()* in the main process (*fsync()* is a system call that tells the OS to flush data to disk). Redis allows you to configure the fsync policy in three possible ways:
    - ° **no**: Do not execute *fsync()*; let the OS decide when to flush the data. *This is the fastest option*
    - ° **always**: Execute *fsync()* after every write. This is the slowest option, but also the safest
    - ° **everysec**: Execute *fsync()* once every second. This still provides good write performance. This is the default value

- **no-appendfsync-on-rewrite**: The possible values are **yes** and **no**. If the **appendfsync** policy is set to **everysec** or **always** and a background save or AOF log rewrite is taking place, Redis may block due to a lot of disk I/O (the *fsync()* syscall will be long). You should only enable this option if you have latency problems. The default value is **no**

- **auto-aof-rewrite-percentage**: The valid values range from 0 to 100. Redis is able to automatically rewrite the log file by implicitly executing the command **BGREWRITEAOF** when the AOF size grows by the specified percentage. The default value is *100*

- **auto-aof-rewrite-min-size**: This is the minimum size for AOF to be rewritten. This prevents AOF rewrites until the specified minimum size is reached, even if the specified **auto-aof-rewrite-percentage** value is exceeded. The default value is 67,108,864 bytes

- **aof-load-truncated**: The possible values are **yes** and **no**. In the event of a crash, the AOF may get truncated, and this option specifies whether Redis should load the truncated AOF on startup or exit with an error. When the value is **yes**, Redis will load the truncated file and emit an error message. When it is **no**, Redis will exit with an error and not load the truncated file

- **dir**: This specifies the directory location of the AOF and RDB files

RDB versus AOF

Restoring data from an RDB is faster than AOF when recovering a big dataset. This is because an RDB does not need to re-execute every change made in the entire database; it only needs to load the data that was previously stored. For instance, imagine that you have a key called *pageview* and it starts with a value of 1. Suppose that a day has passed and now the value of *pageview* is 100000 (since you had this number of visits and the command **INCR** was executed for each visit). If you have to restore your database using AOF, Redis will execute 100,000 **INCR** commands to get the last value of the key. But when restoring using RDB, Redis will create a key with a value of 100000 right away, which is much faster.

Although RDB and AOF are different strategies, they can be enabled at the same time.

Redis will load RDB or AOF on startup if any of the files exists. If both files exist, the AOF takes precedence because of its durability guarantees.

The following are some considerations when using persistence in Redis:

- If your application does not need persistence, disable RDB and AOF
- If your application has tolerance to data loss, use RDB
- If your application requires fully durable persistence, use both RDB and AOF

Replication

Replication means that while you write to a Redis instance (usually referred to as the master), it will ensure that one or more instances (usually referred to as the slaves) become exact copies of the master.

Redis 2.8 introduced asynchronous replication, which makes slaves periodically acknowledge the amount of data to be processed. As you would expect, a master can have multiple slaves and slaves can also accept connections from other slaves.

There are three ways of making a Redis server instance a slave:

- Add the directive **slaveof** IP PORT to the configuration file and start a Redis server using this configuration
- Use the **redis-server** command-line option **--slaveof** IP PORT
- Use the command **SLAVEOF** IP PORT

The following example starts three Redis instances: one master and two replicas.

On the first terminal, start the master **redis-server** on port *5555*:

```
$ redis-server --port 5555
```

On the second terminal, start the first slave on port *6666*:

```
$ redis-server --port 6666 --slaveof 127.0.0.1 5555
```

On the third terminal, start the second slave on port *7777*:

```
$ redis-server --port 7777 --slaveof 127.0.0.1 5555
```

At this point, there is a master with two replicas running.

On the fourth terminal, check whether the replication is working:

```
$ redis-cli -p 5555 SET testkey testvalue
OK
$ redis-cli -p 6666 GET testkey
"testvalue"
$ redis-cli -p 7777 GET testkey
"testvalue"
```

Replicas are widely used for scalability purposes so that all read operations are handled by replicas and the master handles only write operations.

Data redundancy is another reason for having multiple replicas.

Persistence can be moved to the replicas so that the master does not perform disk I/O operations. In this scenario, the master server needs to disable persistence, and it should not restart automatically for any reason; otherwise, it will restart with an empty dataset and replicate it to the replicas, making them delete all of their stored data.

Note:
Replicas are read-only by default, but this can be changed by setting the configuration slave-read-only to yes. This, however, is not recommended!

It is possible to improve data consistency guarantees by requiring a minimum number of replicas connected to the master server. In this way, all write operations are only executed in the master Redis server if the minimum number of replicas are satisfied, along with their maximum replication lag (in seconds). However, this feature is still weak because it does not guarantee that all replicas have accepted the write operations; it only guarantees that there is a minimum number of replicas connected to the master. The configurations use to set it up are **min-slaves-to-write** and **min-slaves-max-lag** — they default to 0 and 10, respectively.

Replicas are very useful in a master failure scenario because they contain all of the most recent data and can be promoted to master. Unfortunately, when Redis is running in single-instance mode, there is no automatic failover to promote a slave to master. All replicas and clients connected to the old master need to be reconfigured with the new master. The automatic failover feature is the core of Redis Sentinel, which is covered in *Chapter 9, Redis Cluster and Redis Sentinel (Collective Intelligence)*.

The command **SLAVEOF NO ONE** converts a slave into a master instance, and it should be used in a failover scenario.

The next example assumes there is a master on port 5555 and there are two slaves on ports 6666 and 7777, respectively. If the master instance is offline (crashed or maintenance window), it may be required that one of its replicas become a master. In this situation, all connected replicas and clients need to be reconfigured.

The following snippet causes a crash in the master instance (port 5555), configures one of the slaves to become a master, and reconfigures the second slave to replicate the new master:

```
$ redis-cli -p 5555 DEBUG SEGFAULT
$ redis-cli -p 6666 SLAVEOF NO ONE
$ redis-cli -p 7777 SLAVEOF 127.0.0.1 6666
```

Check the new replication configuration is working:

```
$ redis-cli -p 6666 SET newkey newvalue
OK
$ redis-cli -p 7777 GET newkey
"newvalue"
```

In the previous scenario, all clients that were connected to *127.0.0.1:5555* need to be reconfigured to connect to *127.0.0.1:6666*.

Partitioning

Partitioning is a general term used to describe the act of breaking up data and distributing it across different hosts. There are two types of partitioning: horizontal partitioning and vertical partitioning. Partitioning is performed in a cluster of hosts when better performance, maintainability, or availability is desired.

When Redis was initially designed, it had no intention to be a distributed data store; thus, it cannot natively distribute its data among different instances. It was designed to work well on a single server. Redis Cluster is designed to solve distributed problems in Redis.

Over time, Redis storage may grow to such an extent that a single server may not be enough to store all of the data. The performance of reading from and writing to a single server may also decline.

As we saw in the previous section, we can use replicas to optimize reads and remove some bottlenecks from the master instance, but in many cases, this is not enough. Different needs require different approaches, and here are some situations that we did not provide information on how to handle yet:

- The total data to be stored is larger than the total memory available in a Redis server
- The network bandwidth is not enough to handle all of the traffic

We will show some solutions to the problems listed in the preceding list using the concept of partitioning. We also will show some client-level implementations of partitioning (in single-instance mode, Redis does not support partitioning or clustering), and later, we will see how it can be done with a proxy or a query routing system. Redis Cluster will be explained in detail in *Chapter 9, Redis Cluster and Redis Sentinel (Collective Intelligence)*.

In the context of Redis, horizontal partitioning means distributing keys across different Redis instances, while vertical partitioning means distributing key values across different Redis instances. For example, if you have two Redis Sets stored in Redis, horizontal partitioning would distribute each Set entirely to a different Redis instance, while vertical partitioning would distribute the Set's values to different instances. Each kind of partitioning has its purpose. Horizontal partitioning (also known as sharding) is the most popular approach adopted with Redis, and it is what we will present in the next section.

Range partitioning

Range partitioning is very simple; data is distributed based on a range of keys. Assuming that the keys you want to partition are based on incremental IDs, you can create numerical ranges to partition the data. For example, assuming that you have a group of users identified by IDs (such as *user:1*, *user:2*, and so on up to *user:5000*) you can split these IDs into ranges of thousands. Then you can send keys that go from 1 to 1000 to a given instance, 1001 to 2000 to a different instance, 2001 to 3000 to another instance, and so on.

A different approach would be to partition the data based on the first letter of each key, so you would send all keys that go from *A* to *G* to one instance, *H* to *O* to another instance, and *P* to *Z* to a third instance. This logic would partition the data into three ranges, and each range would be stored in a different host.

The whole idea of range partitioning is to create ranges of keys and distribute them to different Redis instances. You can be creative in how you create the range selection.

A downside to this type of partitioning is that the distributions will probably be uneven—one range may be much larger than others. For example, if you decide to distribute the keys based on their first letter but you do not have a good distribution of key names (that is, most of your keys are in the same range or some ranges have very few keys), you are going to end up with a very uneven distribution that does not take full advantage of partitioning.

Another downside is that this does not accommodate changing the list of Redis hosts easily, because if the number of Redis instances changes, the range distribution needs to change accordingly. It is likely that adding or removing a host will invalidate a good portion of data.

We are going to demonstrate how to implement range partitioning by distributing keys based on the first character of the key name. You can use this implementation as a reference and create your own range partitioning selection.

A basic implementation of partitioning, which we will extend later, is presented next.

Create a file *partitioning.js* in the *chapter 8* folder with the following code:

```
function Partitioning(clients) { // 1
    this.clients = clients;
}

Partitioning.prototype = {
    _getClient: function(key) { // 2
        throw "Subclass should implement _getClient() method";
    },
    set: function(key, value) { // 3
        var client = this._getClient(key); // 4
        client.set.apply(client, arguments); // 5
    },
    get: function(key) { // 6
        var client = this._getClient(key);
        client.get.apply(client, arguments);
    }
};
module.exports = Partitioning; // 7
```

1. Create a function called *Partitioning*, which will be used later as a base class.

2. Define the method *_getClient()*, which all subclasses will overwrite.

3. Define the method *set()*, which uses the proper client defined by the subclass.

4. Find the right Redis client based on the subclass implementation.

5. Call the method *set()* in the proper client, applying all the arguments that were passed to *set()*, even if they were not present in the function signature.

6. This has the same logic as the *set()* method, but it is meant for **GET**. This is how all other supported Redis commands will be implemented.

7. Export the function *Partitioning* to any other module that calls *require("partitioning")*.

The preceding implementation is very basic and does not implement all Redis commands. It only implements **SET** and **GET**, but it is very easy to extend these commands and add support to more commands. We will use the built-in utilities of Node.js for inheritance to implement all the partitioning methods described in this chapter.

Based on the preceding implementation, we are going to create *RangePartitioning*, a subclass of *Partitioning* that must overwrite the *_getClient()* method:

```
var util = require("util"); // 1
var Partitioning = require("partitioning"); // 2

function RangePartitioning(clients) { // 3
  Partitioning.call(this, clients); // 4
}

util.inherits(RangePartitioning, Partitioning); // 5

RangePartitioning.prototype._getClient = function(key) { // 6
  var possibleValues = '0123456789abcdefghijklmnopqrstuvwxyz';// 7
  var rangeSize = possibleValues.length / this.clients.length;
// 8

  for (var i = 0, clientIndex = 0 ; i < possibleValues.length ;
    i += rangeSize, clientIndex++) { // 9
    var range = possibleValues.slice(i, i + rangeSize); // 10

    if (range.indexOf(key[0].toLowerCase()) != -1) { // 11
      return this.clients[clientIndex]; // 12
    }
  }
  // if key does not start with 0 to 9 neither A to Z,
  // fall back to always using the first client
  return this.clients[0]; // 13
};
```

1. Require the module *util* from the Node.js standard library.

2. Require the module we defined previously in order to use the *Partitioning* base class.

3. Define the function *RangePartitioning*, which will receive the Redis clients.

4. Initialize the function via *Partitioning*. This is a superclass initialization.

5. Create the inheritance between *RangePartitioning* and *Partitioning*.

6. Overwrite the *_getClient()* method in order to define the range partitioning algorithm.

7. The partitions created will be based on alphanumeric characters. All keys that start with other characters are going to fall back to the first Redis client.

8. Define the range size based on the total count of alphanumeric characters and the number of available Redis clients. This will create balanced ranges.

9. Iterate over all alphanumeric characters in order to find the proper client based on a range.

10. Define the range of characters that the Redis key would belong to.

11. Check whether the Redis key starts with the current alphanumeric character.

12. If the previous check is true, it means that the range is correct and it returns the proper Redis client.

Hash partitioning

Hash partitioning is a little more elaborate than range partitioning, and it does not have the range partitioning method's downside of uneven data partitioning. Hash partitioning is very well known, and everyone who manages *Memcached* at scale is familiar with it.

Hash partitioning is very simple to implement. It consists of finding the instance to send the commands by applying a hash function to the Redis key, dividing this hash value by the number of Redis instances available, and using the remainder of that division as the instance index.

A JavaScript snippet may exemplify this idea better than English:

```
var index = hashFunction(redisKey) % redisHosts.length;
var host = redisHosts[index];
```

The efficiency of this method varies with the hash function you choose. If your hash function is good for your dataset, it will create even partitions. It is very common for people to use MD5 and SHA1 as hash functions.

It is recommended to have a prime number as the total number of Redis instances with this partitioning method in order to minimize collisions. If the total number of Redis instances is not a prime number, collisions are more likely to occur.

Create a file called *hashpartitioning.js* in the *chapter 8* folder with the following code:

```
var util = require("util");
var crypto = require('crypto'); // 1
var Partitioning = require("partitioning");

function HashPartitioning(clients) {
  Partitioning.call(this, clients);
}

util.inherits(HashPartitioning, Partitioning);

HashPartitioning.prototype._getClient = function(key) { // 2
  var index = this._hashFunction(key) % this.clients.length;// 3
  return this.clients[index]; // 4
};

HashPartitioning.prototype._hashFunction = function(str) { // 5
  var hash = crypto.createHash('md5').update(str).digest('hex');
// 6
  return parseInt(hash, 16); // 7
};
```

1. Require the module *crypto* from the standard library.
2. Overwrite *_getClient()* to create the hash partitioning logic.
3. Call *_hashFunction()*, passing a Redis key, and use modulo to find the right index in the array of clients.
4. Return the proper client to send the Redis commands.
5. Define the method *_hashFunction()*, which expects a string as the argument.
6. Calculate the MD5 hash of the passed-in string using the *crypto* library. Then return its hexadecimal value.
7. Convert the MD5 hash from string to integer. MD5 is hexadecimal, so 16 is the base in *parseInt()*.

This partitioning method can result in cache misses if the number of instances is changed. If the instance list stays the same size forever, this problem does not occur, which is unlikely to happen because resource failure should be expected.

 In a small test, using hash partitioning, 75 percent of our dataset was invalidated by adding two more servers to the list.

Presharding

One way of dealing with the problem of adding/replacing nodes over time with hash partitioning is to *preshard* the data. This means pre-partitioning the data to a high extent so that the host list size never changes. The idea is to create more Redis instances, reuse the existing servers, and launch more instances on different ports. This works well because Redis is single threaded and does not use all the resources available in the machine, so you can launch many Redis instances per server and still be fine.

Then, with this new list of Redis instances, you would apply the same Hash algorithm that we presented before, but now with far more elements in the Redis client array. This method works because if you need to add more capacity to the cluster, you can replace some Redis instances with more powerful ones, and the client array size never changes.

Let's say we have three Redis servers that we want to use the presharding method on. The client list would look like this:

```
var redisHosts = [
    'server1:6379',
    'server1:6380',
    'server1:6381',
    'server1:6382',
    'server1:6383',

    'server2:6379',
    'server2:6380',
    'server2:6381',
    'server2:6382',
    'server2:6383',

    'server3:6379',
    'server3:6380',
    'server3:6381',
    'server3:6382',
    'server3:6383',
];
```

We chose to have only five instances per server as an example, but some people have over 100 instances per server.

If we decide that *server3* is not capable enough to handle the load, it can be replaced by another server with more capacity, such as *server4*. The steps would be as follows:

1. Launch *server4* with the same number of Redis instances as *server3*. Make each new instance a replica of one of the instances of server3 to avoid losing data.

2. After the synchronization is done in all the new instances, replace all *server3* instances with *server4* instances in the Redis host list.

3. Stop all processes that connect to *server3* instances. Promote *server4* instances to master instances (the **SLAVEOF NO ONE** command).

4. Restart all processes that were previously stopped.

5. Shut down *server3*.

If you cannot afford to stop all processes at once, set the slaves to be writable (**CONFIG SET slave-read-only no**), move all clients to the new instances, and then promote a slave to master.

These ideas are also valid if you want to add more capacity to the cluster. You can always replace a small portion of instances with more powerful instances. The more the instances you have per server, the easier the scaling of the cluster.

The presharding method does not work so well in disaster scenarios. If a group of servers is experiencing issues and the servers need to be replaced, the only way to ensure that the cluster stays balanced is to replace those damaged servers with other servers. By definition, the size of the cluster cannot vary. In a situation like this, clients will try to connect to bad servers, and if new servers are not brought up very quickly, it may have a major impact on the concerned projects. This is not an elastic approach, and as everyone moves to a cloud environment, elasticity is always good to have.

Another downside to this method is that you get significantly more instances to manage and monitor, and unfortunately, there is no great set of tools for doing this. There are other alternatives to this method, and one of them is consistent hashing, which is widely used.

Consistent hashing

We explained how hash partitioning works before. Its main downside is that adding or removing nodes from the list of servers may have a negative impact on key distribution and creation. If Redis is used as a cache system with hash partitioning, it becomes very hard to scale up because the size of the list of Redis servers cannot change (otherwise, a lot of cache misses will happen).

Some researchers at MIT were trying to solve the problem with hash partitioning and caching that we just described, and they came up with the concept of consistent hashing. They wanted a different technique to route keys that would affect only a small portion of data when the hash table was resized.

Consistent hashing, in our context, is a kind of hashing that remaps only a small portion of the data to different servers when the list of Redis servers is changed (only K/n keys are remapped, where K is the number of keys and n is the number of servers).

For example, in a cluster with 100 keys and four servers, adding a fifth node would remap only 25 keys on an average (100 divided by 4). Consistent hashing is also known as a hash ring.

The technique consists of creating multiple points in a circle for each Redis key and server. The appropriate server for a given key is the closest server to that key in the circle (clockwise); this circle is also referred to as "ring." The points are created using a hash function, such as *MD5*.

In order to understand the next examples, assume the following:

- Servers available: *server-1*, *server-2*, and *server-3*
- Key to be stored: *testkey-1*, *testkey-2*, *testkey-3*, and *testkey-4*
- Points per server: 1

Assume that there is a hash function that returns the following values for the servers:

```
hash("server-1") = 3
hash("server-2") = 7
hash("server-3") = 11
```

The same hash function returns the following values for the keys:

```
hash("testkey-1") = 3
hash("testkey-2") = 4
hash("testkey-3") = 8
hash("testkey-4") = 12
```

The following diagram shows the circle with the previous hashes:

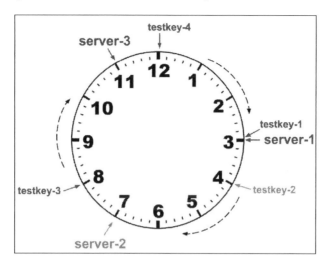

In this hypothetical example, the mapping is as follows:

- *testkey-1* maps to *server-1*. They have to the same value of 3.
- *testkey-2* maps to *server-2*. This is the next server available with a value greater than or equal to 4, and the key distribution moves clockwise.
- *testkey-3* maps to *server-3*. This is the next server available with a value greater than or equal to 8, moving clockwise again.
- *testkey-4* maps to *server-1*. There is no server with a hash greater than or equal to 12. Thus, *testkey-4* falls back to the first node in the ring.

The previous example shows how consistent hashing can be used to route Redis keys to a cluster of Redis servers (the hash values are hypothetical and are meant only to exemplify the concept).

In the real world, it is better to use multiple points for each server, because that way it is easier to distribute keys and keep the ring balanced. Some libraries use as few as three points per server, while others use as many as 500.

The following code implements this technique by creating *ConsistentHashingPartitioning* as a subclass of *Partitioning*:

```
var util = require("util");
var crypto = require("crypto");
var Partitioning = require("partitioning");
```

```
function ConsistentHashingPartitioning(clients, vnodes) { // 1
  this._vnodes = vnodes || 256; // 2
  this._ring = {}; // 3
  this._setUpRing(clients); // 4
}

util.inherits(ConsistentHashingPartitioning, Partitioning); // 5

ConsistentHashingPartitioning.prototype._getClient = function(key) {
// 6
  var ringHashes = Object.keys(this._ring); // 7
  var keyHash = this._hashFunction(key); // 8
  ringHashes.sort(); // 9
  for (var i = 0 ; i < ringHashes.length ; i++) { // 10
    var ringHash = ringHashes[i]; // 11
    if (ringHash >= keyHash) { // 12
      return this._ring[ringHash]; // 13
    }
  }
  // fallback to the start of the ring
  return this._ring[ringHashes[0]]; // 14
};

ConsistentHashingPartitioning.prototype._hashFunction = function(str)
{ // 15
  return crypto.createHash('md5').update(str).digest('hex');
};

ConsistentHashingPartitioning.prototype._setUpRing =
  function(clients) { // 16
  for (var i = 0 ; i < clients.length; i++) {
    this.addClient(clients[i]);
  }
};

ConsistentHashingPartitioning.prototype.addClient =
  function(client) { // 17
    for (var i = 0 ; i < this._vnodes ; i++) { // 18
      var hash = this._hashFunction(client.address + ":" + i);
// 19
      this._ring[hash] = client; // 20
    }
};
```

```
ConsistentHashingPartitioning.prototype.removeClient =
  function(client) { // 21
  for (var i = 0 ; i < this._vnodes ; i++) {
    var hash = this._hashFunction(client.address + ":" + i);
    delete this._ring[hash];
  }
};
```

1. Create *ConsistentHashPartitioning*, which should receive the List of clients and the number of virtual nodes per client (the number of replicated points in the ring).

2. Assign the number of passed-in virtual nodes that defaults to *256* if no value is passed in.

3. Initialize the ring as an empty object. This ring object is going to be used as a hash.

4. Set up the ring based on the clients passed in as parameters.

5. Make *ConsistentHashPartitioning* a subclass of *Partitioning*.

6. Overwrite the method *_getClient()*.

7. Get all keys of the ring (the keys are the hash values assigned to each server).

8. Create a hash for the key passed as a parameter.

9. Sort the ring hashes. This will make comparison easier.

10. Iterate over the sorted ring hashes.

11. Assign *ringHash* to the appropriate index. This value is a hexadecimal string.

12. Compare the current ring hash with the key hash value; if the ring hash is greater than or equal to the key hash, it means that this is the right server. This logic is correct because *ringHashes* is sorted.

13. Return the Redis client in the *ringHash* position of the ring.

14. If all the values of the ring are not enough to find the key hash, fall back to the first node in the ring.

15. Define *_hashFunction()* to return the MD5 of any string, in hexadecimal form rather than in decimal form. The return value looks like *0e2332b21bb0e972520765a2c18ea281*.

16. Define *_setUpRing()* to call *addClient()* for each of the client passed in the *ConsistentHashingPartitioning* constructor.

17. Define *addClient()*.

18. Iterate over the number of virtual nodes that should be created for each client.

19. For each server, create a hash value based on the string concatenation of the client address, the colon, and the virtual node index.

20. Assign the current client to the ring using the hash created in the previous step.

21. Define *removeClient()* to be the opposite of *addClient()*. This method and *addClient()* are useful for managing the client List without recreating objects.

Tagging

Tagging is a technique of ensuring that keys are stored on the same server. Choose a convention for your key names and add a prefix or suffix. Then decide how to route that key based on the added prefix or suffix. The convention in the Redis community is to add a tag to a key name with the tag name inside curly braces (that is, *key_ name:{tag}*).

Commands such as **SDIFF, SINTER,** and **SUNION** require that all keys are stored in the same Redis instance in order to work. One way of guaranteeing that the keys will be stored in the same Redis instance is by using tagging.

Here are some examples that would hash to the same value:

- *user:1{users}*
- *user:2{users}*
- *user:3{users}*

The following code changes *ConsistentHashingPartitioning* to add tagging support:

```
ConsistentHashingPartitioning.prototype._hashFunction = function(str) {
  var stringToHash;
  // match string like "foo{bar}"
  var tagRegex = /.+\{(.+)\}/; // 1
  var regexValues = tagRegex.exec(str); // 2
  if (regexValues === null) { // 3
    stringToHash = str;
  } else { // 4
    stringToHash = regexValues[1];
  }
  return crypto.createHash('md5').update(stringToHash).digest('hex');
// 5
};
```

1. Create a regular expression that matches a string with tags.

2. Apply the key name to the regular expression, and capture the tag name.

3. If the string does not match the tag regular expression, assign *str* to *stringToHash*.

4. If the string matches the tag regular expression, assign the tag value to *stringToHash*.

5. Return an MD5 based on the key name or tag, depending on the previous *if-else* statement.

Data store versus cache

The partitioning ideas presented in this chapter are a great way of scaling Redis and creating a cluster of servers. We recommend consistent hashing as the best partition mechanism, because it gives us the ability to add and remove Redis instances without remapping most of the keys.

When Redis is used as a data store, the keys must always map to the same Redis instances and tagging should be used. Unfortunately, this means that the list of Redis servers cannot change; otherwise, a key could have been able to map to a different Redis instance. One way of solving this is to create copies of the data across Redis instances so that every key is replicated to a number of instances, and the system knows how to route queries (this is similar to how **Riak** stores data). This approach does not work well in a lot of situations, but it does if memory size is not a problem and high availability is desired. It is a lot of work to create that logic by ourselves, and Redis Cluster is meant to solve this kind of problem. *Chapter 9, Redis Cluster and Redis Sentinel (Collective Intelligence)*, will present Redis Cluster in detail.

When Redis is used as a cache, we recommend consistent hashing to minimize cache misses, but any other partitioning method works equally well.

In summary, when Redis is used as a cache, use consistent hashing. When it is used as a data store, consider Redis Cluster or a solution that ensures that data is replicated across nodes and that every instance (or a master instance) knows how to route the query to the right instance.

Implementations of Redis partitioning

Partitioning can be implemented in different layers: client, proxy, or query router.

- The client layer is the application layer, such as what we implemented in the previous examples.

- The proxy layer is an extra layer that proxies all Redis queries and performs partitioning for applications. When a proxy is used, the client layer does not even need to know that partitioning is taking place. An example of this layer is the **twemproxy** program, which we are going to present in the next section.

- The query router layer is something that is invisible to the application. However, it is not an external program; it is the data store itself. Any command issued to any Redis instance will succeed with this layer, because the Redis instance itself will make sure that the command is routed to the appropriate instance in its cluster. Redis Cluster behaves like a query router.

When any form of partitioning is used, not all Redis commands are going to be available; some commands do not make sense in a partitioned system. Commands that inspect the Redis server will not work, because in such cases, a cluster of instances is available instead of just one. Commands that take multiple keys as parameters may not work either, because the keys may be distributed across different hosts.

Automatic sharding with twemproxy

A few techniques of implementing partitioning in Redis were previously presented, such as range partitioning, hash partitioning, presharding, and consistent hashing. This section will introduce a production-ready tool called **twemproxy** (pronounced "two-em-proxy"), which is also known as **nutcracker**. It was created by Twitter, released in 2012, and licensed under Apache License Version 2.0.

twemproxy is a fast and lightweight proxy for Redis and memcached protocols that implements sharding with support for multiple hashing modes, including consistent hashing. It also enables pipelining of requests and responses, and maintains persistent server connections to shard your data automatically across multiple servers. It works on Linux, *BSD, and Smart OS (Solaris). **twemproxy** is a great tool, and it will help us easily scale Redis horizontally. It has been used in production by companies such as Pinterest, Tumblr, Twitter, Vine, Wikimedia, Digg, and Snapchat.

This section shows you how to compile, configure, and use **twemproxy** to connect to three Redis instances, and distribute the writes and reads across those instances.

We will run three different Redis instances to demonstrate how **twemproxy** works. We decided to run them on different ports on the same computer, but nothing prevents you from running them on different servers, such as EC2 instances.

In a new terminal window, run the following commands:

```
$ redis-server --port 6666 --daemonize yes
$ redis-server --port 7777 --daemonize yes
$ redis-server --port 8888 --daemonize yes
```

This will start three Redis servers in the background using ports *6666*, *7777*, and *8888* (if you have any processes running on any of these ports, you should use other values). Open three new terminal windows. Go to each of them and run **redis-cli** to connect to each Redis server:

```
$ redis-cli -p 6666
$ redis-cli -p 7777
$ redis-cli -p 8888
```

Execute the command **MONITOR** in each terminal window and keep them open until the end of this section, as follows:

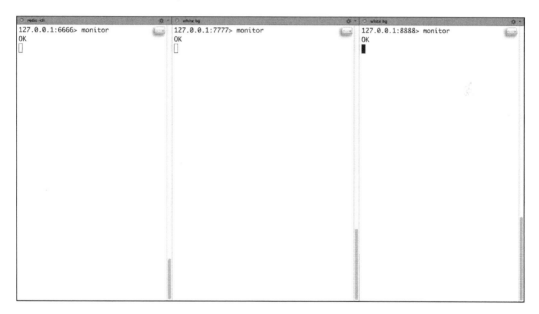

Everything is all set with our Redis server instances. The next steps require downloading and compiling **twemproxy**. Visit https://github.com/twitter/twemproxy, where you can find the documentation about **twemproxy**.

At the time of writing this book, the latest version of the **twemproxy** tarball was *nutcracker-0.4.1.tar.gz*. Download the tarball from the documentation page on GitHub.

Now open a terminal window, navigate to the folder where you downloaded the **twemproxy** tarball, and run the following commands:

```
$ tar -zxf nutcracker-0.4.1.tar.gz
$ cd nutcracker-0.4.1
$ ./configure
$ make
```

This will extract the **nutcracker** files, configure the project, and compile it. If everything went well during the compilation process, you should be able to execute **nutcracker**, which is inside the *src* folder:

```
$ ./src/nutcracker --help
```

As you can see in the following screenshot, the output should list all the available options for configuring **nutcracker**:

```
$ ./src/nutcracker --help
This is nutcracker-0.4.1

Usage: nutcracker [-?hVdDt] [-v verbosity level] [-o output file]
                  [-c conf file] [-s stats port] [-a stats addr]
                  [-i stats interval] [-p pid file] [-m mbuf size]

Options:
  -h, --help              : this help
  -V, --version           : show version and exit
  -t, --test-conf         : test configuration for syntax errors and exit
  -d, --daemonize         : run as a daemon
  -D, --describe-stats    : print stats description and exit
  -v, --verbose=N         : set logging level (default: 5, min: 0, max: 11)
  -o, --output=S          : set logging file (default: stderr)
  -c, --conf-file=S       : set configuration file (default: conf/nutcracker.yml)
  -s, --stats-port=N      : set stats monitoring port (default: 22222)
  -a, --stats-addr=S      : set stats monitoring ip (default: 0.0.0.0)
  -i, --stats-interval=N  : set stats aggregation interval in msec (default: 30000 msec)
  -p, --pid-file=S        : set pid file (default: off)
  -m, --mbuf-size=N       : set size of mbuf chunk in bytes (default: 16384 bytes)
```

We will not explain all the options available in the **nutcracker** command line, most of which are self-explanatory and straightforward, but if you have questions, the documentation is a great resource.

twemproxy is compiled and ready to go, but we need to create a configuration file for it. The file format used by **twemproxy** for configuration is YAML (a recursive acronym for "YAML Ain't Markup Language"). This configuration file has information about the Redis servers that **twemproxy** is going to manage, the hash mode and distribution method that we are going to use, and so on.

Create a new file called *twemproxy_redis.yml* in the *chapter 8* folder with the following code:

```
my_cluster:
  listen: 127.0.0.1:22121
  hash: md5
  distribution: ketama
  auto_eject_hosts: true
  redis: true
  servers:
   - 127.0.0.1:6666:1 server1
   - 127.0.0.1:7777:1 server2
   - 127.0.0.1:8888:1 server3
```

The configuration is now explained line by line:

1. **my_cluster**: This is the name of our **twemproxy** pool configuration.
2. **listen**: These are the IP and port that a Redis client should connect to. This is the bind address of the **twemproxy** cluster.
3. **hash**: This is the hash function that should be used. **twemproxy** supports multiple hashing modes; check out the documentation for more details.
4. **distribution**: This is the distribution mode that should be used (ketama and consistent hashing are the same thing).
5. **redis**: A boolean for defining whether the server pool will be using Redis or Memcached.
6. **servers**: A list of Redis servers using the format **IP:PORT:WEIGHT NAME**.

There are many other options you can use, but to keep this example as simple as possible, we will only cover the basic options.

Recommended reading:

Read `https://github.com/twitter/twemproxy/blob/master/notes/recommendation.md` if you are deploying *nutcracker* in production.

Run nutcracker using the following command:

```
$ ./src/nutcracker -c twemproxy_redis.yml
```

We will create a small JavaScript program that writes each letter of the alphabet as a key in Redis to observe how **twemproxy** distributes the keys across our three Redis instances.

Create a file called *twemproxy.js* in the *chapter 8* folder with the following code:

```
var redis = require('redis');
var options = {   // 1
    "no_ready_check": true,
};
var client = redis.createClient(22121, 'localhost', options); // 2
var alphabet = [
  'A', 'B', 'C', 'D', 'E', 'F', 'G', 'H', 'I',
  'J', 'K', 'L', 'M', 'N', 'O', 'P', 'Q', 'R',
  'S', 'T', 'U', 'V', 'W', 'X', 'Y', 'Z'
]; // 3
alphabet.forEach(function(letter) {   // 4
    client.set(letter, letter);   // 5
});
client.quit();   // 6
```

1. Create an object with a property called *no_ready_check* to avoid the node_redis client from calling the command **INFO** (this command is not supported by **twemproxy**).
2. Create a Redis client and pass the **twemproxy** port and the variable *options*.
3. Create an array with all the letters of the alphabet that will be used as keys and values to be stored in our Redis instances.
4. This creates a simple loop for obtaining each letter of our array.
5. Execute the command **SET** to store each letter as a key and a value in Redis.
6. Close the connection between your Redis client and **twemproxy**.

Execute the file *twemproxy.js*:

```
$ node twemproxy.js
```

Go back to the other three terminal windows with **MONITOR** running so that you can see how **twemproxy** distributes our keys across each Redis instance, as shown in this screenshot:

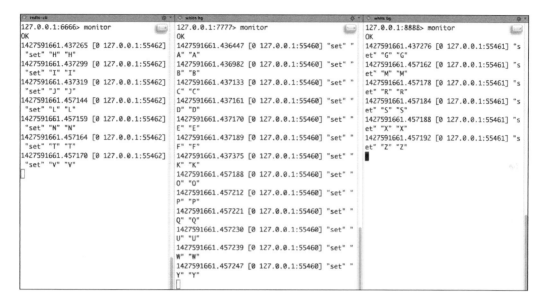

As you can see, **twemproxy** has distributed keys across all existing nodes.

Other architectures that use twemproxy

The example that we created works well, but it makes **twemproxy** a single point of failure. In the event of the **twemproxy** process dying, you will not be able to read or write to any of your Redis server instances, even if they are working fine:

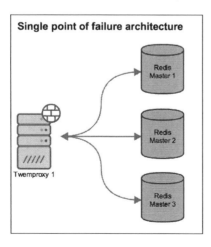

To solve this problem, we could use a different architecture. It has a load balancer in front of a **twemproxy** cluster, and each **twemproxy** cluster is connected to all Redis servers, as follows:

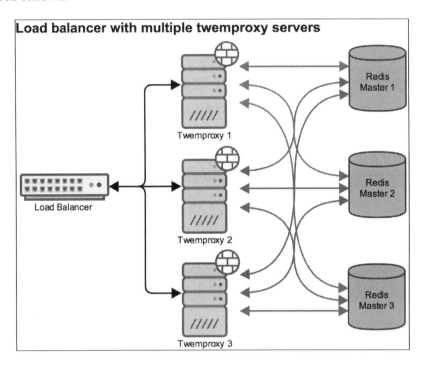

Another possible architecture has **twemproxy** running on the same server as your application, since it is fast and lightweight.

Summary

This chapter introduced persistence, replication using a master and slaves, partitioning methods, presharding, and consistent hashing. It also showed you how to compile and configure **twemproxy** to enable sharding across multiple servers without having to write any code. In the next chapter, we will explain how to use Redis Sentinel and Redis Cluster.

9

Redis Cluster and Redis Sentinel (Collective Intelligence)

Redis was initially designed to be very lightweight and fast. Previously, the only topology available for anyone using Redis was master/slave, in which the master receives all the writes and replicates the changes to the slave (or slaves). This happens without any sort of automatic failover or data sharding. This topology works well in many scenarios, such as when:

- The master has enough memory to store all of the data that you need
- More slaves can be added to scale reads better or when network bandwidth is a problem (the total read volume is higher than the hardware capability)
- It is acceptable to stop your application when maintenance is required on the master machine
- Data redundancy through slaves is enough

But it does not work well in other scenarios, such as when:

- The dataset is bigger than the available memory in the master Redis instance
- A given application cannot be stopped when there are issues with the master instance
- You need to distribute data among multiple nodes
- A single point of failure is not acceptable

In 2011, *Salvatore Sanfilippo* started working on a project that would solve these problems, but Redis was still underdeveloped. He decided to stop his work because of requests from the community to support other features, such as persistence, better data types, introspection, and replication. In 2011, he did not have a lot of knowledge about distributed systems, and Redis Cluster was a complex project to create. It was a great idea, but it required more experience than he had at that time. Solving all of these problems was a difficult task, so he decided to tackle only automatic failover and created a project called Redis Sentinel.

Redis Sentinel and Redis Cluster share a lot of characteristics, but each has its own goal. Sentinel's goal is to provide reliable automatic failover in a master/slave topology without sharding data. Cluster's goal is to distribute data across different Redis instances and perform automatic failover if any problem happens to any master instance.

Redis Sentinel became stable in Redis 2.8 in late 2013, and Redis Cluster became stable in Redis 3.0 in early 2015.

The CAP theorem

Most distributed systems are generally analyzed using the CAP theorem, which states that a distributed system cannot ensure all of the following:

- **Consistency**: A read operation is guaranteed to return the most recent write
- **Availability**: Any operation is guaranteed to receive a response saying whether it has succeeded or failed
- **Partition tolerance**: The system continues to operate when a network partition occurs

Since Redis Sentinel and Redis Cluster are distributed systems, it is fair to analyze them using the CAP theorem. Network partitions are unavoidable in a distributed system, so it should ensure either consistency or availability; that is, it should be either CP or AP.

Theoretically, Redis Sentinel and Redis Cluster are neither consistent nor available under network partitions. However, there are some configurations that can minimize the consistency and availability problems.

They cannot provide availability because there is a quorum that needs to agree on a master election, and depending on the quorum's decision, part of the system may become unavailable.

They cannot provide consistency under network partitions, for example, when two or more partitions accept writes at the same time. When the network heals and the partitions are joined, some of those writes will be lost (conflicts are not automatically solved, nor are they exposed for clients).

Recommended reading:
Read the CAP FAQ at `http://henryr.github.io/cap-faq/`.

Redis Sentinel

When a master node experiences issues, one of its slave nodes needs to be promoted to master, and all the other slaves need to be reconfigured to point to the new master. Before Redis Sentinel, this failover process was done manually, which was not very reliable.

Redis Sentinel is a distributed system designed to automatically promote a Redis slave to master if the existing master fails. Sentinel does not distribute data across nodes since the master node has all of the data and the slaves have a copy of the data—Sentinel is not a distributed data store.

The most common architecture contains an installation of one Sentinel for each Redis server. Sentinel is a separate process from the Redis server, and it listens on its own port.

If a firewall is configured in your setup, it needs to allow Sentinel to connect to all other Sentinels and Redis servers in the group.

If your architecture has one master and two replicas, you can use Sentinel in the following way:

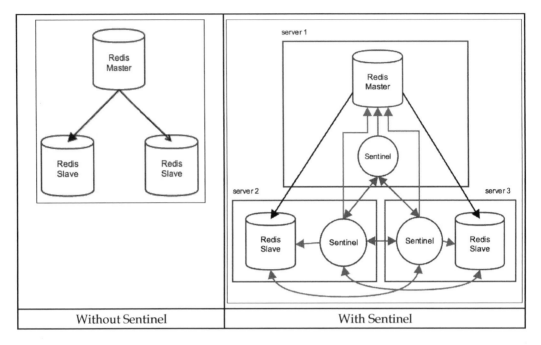

| Without Sentinel | With Sentinel |

The major difference when using Redis Sentinel is that it implements a different interface, which may require you to install a Redis client that supports Sentinel.

A client always connects to a Redis instance, but it needs to query a Sentinel to find out what Redis instance it is going to connect to.

When you download Redis, it comes with a configuration file for Sentinel, called *sentinel.conf*. In the initial configuration, only the master nodes need to be listed. All slaves are found when Sentinel starts and asks the masters where their slaves are. The Sentinel configuration will be rewritten as soon as the Sentinel finds all the available slaves, or when a failover occurs.

Communication between all Sentinels takes place through a Pub/Sub channel called __**sentinel__:hello** in the Redis master.

The basic Sentinel configuration

A Redis Sentinel configuration will always monitor a master identified by an IP and a port and have a name identification. This will be the name of your group of sentinels. In the following example, the name is *mymaster*:

```
sentinel monitor mymaster 127.0.0.1 6379 2
sentinel down-after-milliseconds mymaster 30000
sentinel failover-timeout mymaster 180000
sentinel parallel-syncs mymaster 1
```

The preceding configuration monitors a Redis master with the name *mymaster*, IP address *127.0.0.1*, port *6379*, and quorum *2*. The quorum represents the fewest number of sentinels that need to agree that the current master is down before starting a new master election.

A Sentinel will only notify other Sentinels that its master is down after the master is unreachable (unable to reply a **PING**) for a given number of milliseconds, specified in the directive **down-after-milliseconds**.

The sentinel configuration is rewritten every time a new master is elected or a new sentinel or slave joins the group of instances. The directive **down-after-milliseconds** is also used to update the configuration with the current list of slaves and sentinels, following the same rule explained in the previous paragraph.

The main purpose of the directive **failover-timeout** is to avoid a failover to a master that has experienced issues in a short period of time (which is specified via the **failover-timeout** directive). For example, assume that there is a master, R1, with three slaves, R2, R3, and R4. If the master experiences issues, the slaves need to elect a new master. Assume that R2 becomes the new master and R1 returns to the group as a slave. If R2 has issues and another new election must take place before **failover-timeout** is exceeded, R1 will not be part of the possible nodes to be elected as the master.

The last directive in the preceding configuration is **parallel-syncs**, which specifies the number of slaves that can be reconfigured simultaneously to point to a new master. During this process the slaves will be unavailable to clients. Use a low **parallel-syncs** number to minimize the number of simultaneously unavailable slaves.

Connecting to Sentinel

Here is an example that shows how to connect to Redis Sentinel, from the official Ruby Redis client:

```
SENTINELS = [
    {:host => "127.0.0.1", :port => 26380},
    {:host => "127.0.0.1", :port => 26381}
]
redis = Redis.new(:url => "redis://mymaster", :sentinels => SENTINELS,
:role => :master)
```

This code tries to connect to one of the sentinels in the *SENTINELS* array. The client will try to connect to the first sentinel. If this sentinel is down, it tries to connect to the next, and so on. The *role* parameter is responsible for defining whether the client will connect to the master or to a random slave in a given group (the master's name is specified in the *url* parameter). The available values for the *role* parameter are *:master* and *:slave*.

Network partition (split-brain)

Redis Sentinel is not strongly consistent in a network partition scenario. Data may be lost when a split-brain occurs. *Kyle Kingsbury* (also known as **Aphyr** on the Internet) wrote some very detailed blog posts on Redis Sentinel and its lack of consistency. The last post can be found at `https://aphyr.com/posts/287-asynchronous-replication-with-failover`. *Salvatore Sanfilippo* (also known as **Antirez**) wrote a reply to that blog post, which can be found at `http://antirez.com/news/56`.

To demonstrate how Redis Sentinel will lose data when a split-brain occurs, assume the following:

- There are three Redis instances: one master and two replicas. For each Redis instance, there is a Redis Sentinel
- There is a client connected to the current master and writing to it

If a network partition occurs and separates the current master from all of its slaves, and the slaves can still talk to each other, one of the slaves will be promoted to master.

Meanwhile, the client will continue to write to the isolated master.

If the network heals and all the servers are able to communicate to each other again, the majority of sentinels will agree that the old master (the one that was isolated) should become a slave of the new master (the slave that was promoted to master). When this happens, all writes sent by the client are lost, because there is no data synchronization in this process.

The architecture before split-brain is as follows:

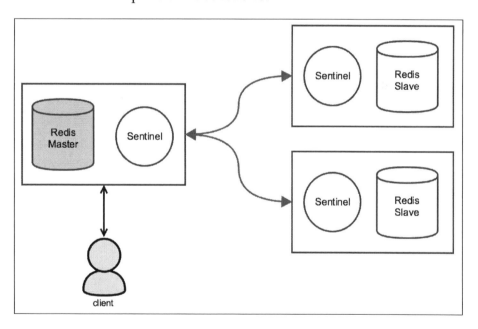

And the architecture after split-brain is as shown here:

Redis Sentinel solves the automatic failover problem of high availability, but it does not solve the problem of distributing data across multiple Redis instances. Redis Cluster solves both of these problems with a different approach, which we will cover in the next sections.

Redis Cluster

Redis Cluster was designed to automatically shard data across different Redis instances, providing some degree of availability during network partitions. It is not strongly consistent under chaotic scenarios.

Unlike Sentinel, Redis Cluster only requires a single process to run. However, there are two ports that Redis uses. The first is used to serve clients (low port), and the second serves as a bus for node-to-node communication (high port). The high port is used to exchange messages such as failure detection, failover, resharding, and so on.

The Redis Cluster bus uses a binary protocol to exchange messages between nodes. The low port is specified in the configuration, and Redis assigns the high port by adding 10,000 to the low port. For example, if a Redis server starts listening to port 6379 (low port) in cluster mode, it will internally assign port *16379* (high port) for node-to-node communication. The Redis Cluster topology is a full mesh network. All nodes are interconnected through **Transmission Control Protocol** (**TCP**) connections.

Redis Cluster requires at least three masters, as shown in the following figure, to be considered healthy. All data is sharded across the masters and replicated to the slaves:

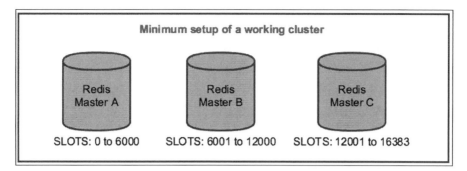

It is recommended that you have at least one replica per master. Otherwise, if any master node without at least one replica fails, the data will be lost:

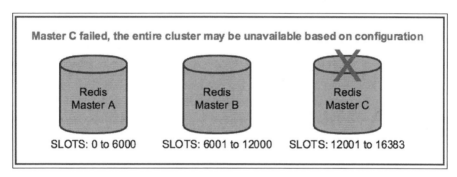

Unlike Redis Sentinel, when a failover is happening in Redis Cluster, only the keys in the slots assigned to the failed master are unavailable until a replica is promoted. The data may be unavailable during a failover, because slave promotion is not instantaneous.

When Redis is in cluster mode, its interface is slightly changed. This requires a smarter client. When connecting to Redis through **redis-cli**, the **-c** parameter is required to enable cluster mode. Otherwise, Redis will work in single-instance mode:

```
$ redis-cli -c -h localhost -p 6379
```

Hash slots

The partitioning method used to shard data by Redis Cluster is similar to the hash partitioning method described in *Chapter 8, Scaling Redis (Beyond a Single Instance)*, but the method is always applied on top of a fixed value. In Redis Cluster, that fixed value is *16,384*. Redis calls this method **hash slot**. Each master in a cluster owns a portion of the 16,384 slots.

The hash slot is found by using the *CRC-16* hash function to convert the key into an integer, and then calculating modulo 16,384 of that integer. The following pseudocode illustrates how a hash slot is calculated for a given key:

```
HASH_SLOT = CRC16(key) mod 16384
```

Take the following into consideration:

- A master without any slots assigned to it will not be able store data. A client connected to this master will be redirected to another master for any query
- A master should have at least one slot. Otherwise, no keys will be routed to it
- The total number of slots allocated must be 16,384 across all masters
- There is no automatic redistribution of slots for masters. You need to manually assign x number of slots to each master

Hash tags

Any multi-key operations require all keys to be stored in the same node, and hash tags are the only way to ensure this in Redis Cluster. This is very similar to what we presented with **twemproxy**. A hash tag is used to apply the hash function and ensure that different key names end up in the same hash slot. If you need to store information about a user, identified by an ID, you can change your key names to be something similar to the following:

```
SADD {user123}:friends:usa "John" "Bob"
SADD {user123}:friends:brazil "Max" "Hugo"
SUNION {user123}:all_friends {user123}:friends:usa
{user123}:friends:brazil
```

In this way, all keys will be stored in the same slot, based on the hash tag **user123** (delimited by curly braces).

Creating a basic cluster

When Redis is downloaded, it comes with a **create-cluster** shell script inside the *utils/create-cluster* directory. We are going to use this script to create a basic cluster so as to get familiarized with some features and concepts that we will approach in the next sections. We will cover more details on how to create and configure clusters later in this chapter. Managing a cluster requires a lot of steps. To make this task easier, Redis distributes a utility called **redis-trib**, which has a very straightforward interface. Behind the scenes, **redis-trib** executes Redis commands on instances to add nodes to a cluster, remove nodes from a cluster, distribute hash slots, check the cluster health, and so on.

Use the **create-cluster start** command to initialize six Redis instances (assuming that Redis was installed from source, as recommended in *Chapter 1, Getting Started (The Baby Steps)*):

```
$ cd /path/to/redis-3.0.2/utils/create-cluster/
$ ./create-cluster start
Starting 30001
Starting 30002
Starting 30003
Starting 30004
Starting 30005
Starting 30006
```

After the instances are up and running, we are going to run the **create** command to create a cluster with all the instances that we initialized in the previous step. The **create-cluster** script creates a cluster with one replica for each master (three replicas total). A prompt will ask you how you want the hash slot distribution. By default, it distributes them evenly across all masters. You can reply **yes** to accept this default configuration. The output should be similar to this (assuming that the *redis* gem was installed, as recommended in *Chapter 5, Clients for Your Favorite Language (Become a Redis Polyglot)*):

```
$ ./create-cluster create
... # output omitted
M: bfe5766a6c75729fba842add9fa05f9fddda128c 127.0.0.1:30001
   slots:0-5460 (5461 slots) master
M: 0d4ae9e8d6e3150920030774e3a3fa4584578cd3 127.0.0.1:30002
   slots:5461-10922 (5462 slots) master
M: da73d3f09aa544f154e48854a3cf8372822134e1 127.0.0.1:30003
   slots:10923-16383 (5461 slots) master
... # output omitted
[OK] All 16384 slots covered.
```

Finding nodes and redirects

A client can connect to any node in a cluster and run queries, but that node may not have the slots required to run a particular query. Thus, the client is responsible for finding the node that has all keys used in that query. After that, it must redirect the connection to the proper node to run the query.

Using the **redis-cli** utility, you can see redirects taking place (this example is based on the cluster created with the **create-cluster** script in the previous section):

```
$ redis-cli -c -h localhost -p 30001
localhost:30001> SET hello world
OK
localhost:30001> SET foo bar
-> Redirected to slot [12182] located at 127.0.0.1:30003
OK
127.0.0.1:30003> GET foo
"bar"
127.0.0.1:30003> GET hello
-> Redirected to slot [866] located at 127.0.0.1:30001
"world"
127.0.0.1:30001>
```

As you can see, the client was initially connected to the Redis master running on port *30001*. The **SET** command was executed to store the key *hello*. As we mentioned before, a key is always routed to a slot using the *CRC-16* hash function and the modulo of 16,384. In this case, no redirect was necessary since the client was connected to the node that had the hash slot assigned to the key *hello*.

Then, another **SET** command was executed to store the key *foo*. This time, a redirect was necessary because a different node had the hash slot necessary to store that key.

The **GET** commands have the same behavior; the client will be redirected to a different node only if necessary.

See the slot distribution across all masters and the calculated hash slots:

```
127.0.0.1:30001 has slots from 0 to 5460
127.0.0.1:30002 has slots from 5461 to 10922
127.0.0.1:30003 has slots from 10923 to 16383

CRC16("hello") % 16834 = 866
CRC16("foo") % 16834 = 12182
```

Configuration

In order to run Redis in cluster mode, you need to specify a new set of directives. Otherwise, it will run as a single-instance server.

The following is an example of a Redis Cluster configuration:

```
cluster-enabled yes
cluster-config-file cluster.conf
cluster-node-timeout 2000
cluster-slave-validity-factor 10
cluster-migration-barrier 1
cluster-require-full-coverage yes
```

The directive **cluster-enabled** is used to determine whether Redis will run in cluster mode or not. But by default, it is **no**. You need to change it to **yes** to enable cluster mode.

Redis Cluster requires a configuration file path to store changes that happen to the cluster. This file path should not be created or edited by humans. The directive that sets this file path is **cluster-config-file**. Redis is responsible for creating this file with all of the cluster information, such as all the nodes in a cluster, their state, and persistence variables. This file is rewritten whenever there is any change in the cluster.

The maximum amount of time for which a node can be unavailable without being considered as failing is specified by the directive **cluster-node-timeout** (this value is in milliseconds). If a node is not reachable for the specified amount of time by the majority of master nodes, it will be considered as failing. If that node is a master, a failover to one of its slaves will occur. If it is a slave, it will stop accepting queries.

Sometimes, network failures happen, and when they happen, it is always a good idea to minimize problems. If network issues are happening and nodes cannot communicate well, it is possible that the majority of nodes think that a given master is down and so a failover procedure should start. If the network only had a hiccup, the failover procedure might have been unnecessary. There is a configuration directive that helps minimize these kinds of problems. The directive is **cluster-slave-validity-factor**, and it expects a factor. By default, the factor is **10**. If there is a network issue and a master node cannot communicate well with other nodes for a certain amount of time (**cluster-node-timeout** multiplied by **cluster-slave-validity-factor**), no slaves will be promoted to replace that master. When the connection issues go away and the master node is able to communicate well with others again, if it becomes unreachable a failover will happen.

When the factor is set to zero, no failovers will be prevented. If any network connectivity issues occur and the factor is zero, a slave will always perform the failover.

It is possible to specify the minimum number of slaves that must be connected to a master through the directive **cluster-migration-barrier**, which has a default value of *1*. This directive is useful if you need to ensure a minimum number of slaves per master. Otherwise, masters without slaves will borrow spare slaves from other masters.

Take the following example: master A has A1 and A2 as slaves, master B has B1 as a slave, master C has C1 as a slave, and the directive **cluster-migration-barrier** is set to 2. If master C fails and C1 gets promoted to master, master A will keep all of its slaves (because the minimum is 2), and master C1 will have zero slaves. If you never want to have masters borrowing slaves from other masters, set this configuration to a high number. The value of *0* is discouraged, since it should be used for debugging only.

In Redis Cluster, all data is sharded among master nodes. If any master node fails and there is no slave to fail over to, a portion of the data will be lost. When this happens, you have two options:

- Make the entire cluster unavailable
- Make the cluster available, but such that all keys that would be routed to that master node will result in an error

The directive that controls this behavior is **cluster-require-full-coverage.** By default, it is **yes**. Full coverage means that all 16,384 hash slots are assigned to reachable masters.

If this directive is set to **yes**, all hash slots must be reachable. Otherwise, the entire cluster will be unavailable. If it is set to **no,** the cluster will still be available, but queries that route to hash slots assigned to any unreachable masters will result in errors.

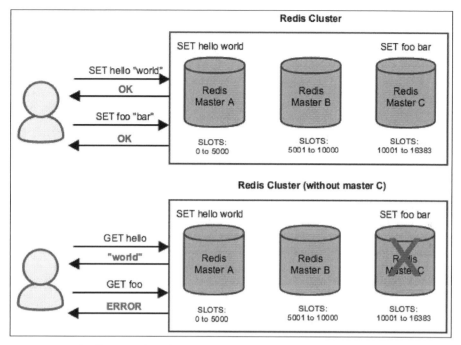

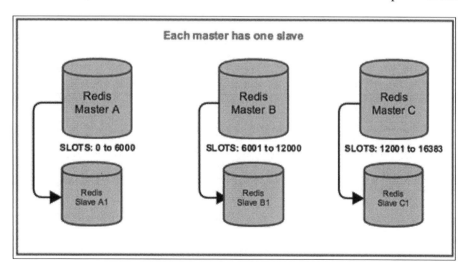

Redis Cluster with configuration **cluster-require-full-coverage** set to *false*

Different Redis Cluster architectures

As we said before, it is recommended that there be at least one slave per master:

The problem with this architecture is that if, for any reason, a master fails, one slave will be promoted to master but will not have any slaves. While the other nodes can fail without causing issues, the master without slaves cannot fail—if it fails, the data will be lost. The following diagram illustrates this scenario. Master C has failed, so slave C1 is promoted to master. If C1 fails, the data will be lost (the cluster may become unavailable if **cluster-require-full-coverage** is set to **yes**):

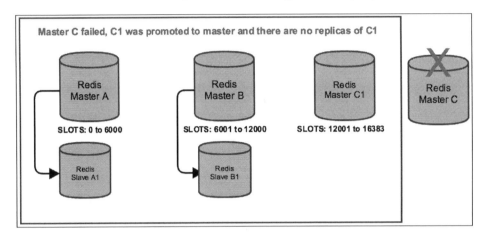

A better architecture would be to have multiple slaves for each master, but that may not be very cost-effective. A safe and cost-effective option is to have spare slaves for some masters in the cluster. In this way, if anything happens to a master with only one slave, the slave is promoted to master. Then one of the spare slaves will become a slave of the new master. In this diagram, master A has two slaves, and every other master has one slave:

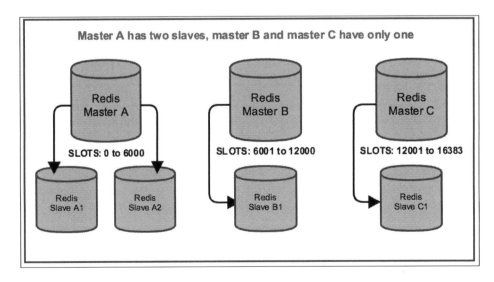

If master C has issues and C1 is promoted to master, as shown in the following diagram, then one of the extra slaves of master A will become a slave of C1 (assuming that **cluster-migration-barrier** is set to *1*):

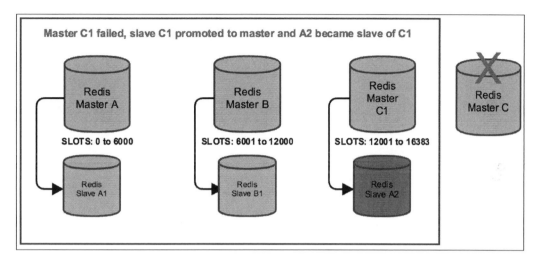

Cluster administration

In the previous sections, we set up a basic Redis Cluster using the **create-cluster** script, explained cluster configuration, presented some essential knowledge about hash slots and failover behaviors, and explained the different cluster architectures. Next, we will show how to create and manage a cluster without any external tools, using only the cluster commands that are existent in Redis.

Creating a cluster

In this section, a cluster with three masters will be created.

The first thing we are going to do is create three Redis instances in cluster mode using the configuration directives presented in the previous section:

```
$ redis-server --port 5000 --cluster-enabled yes --cluster-config-file
nodes-5000.conf --cluster-node-timeout 2000 --cluster-slave-validity-
factor 10 --cluster-migration-barrier 1 --cluster-require-full-coverage
yes --dbfilename dump-5000.rdb  --daemonize yes
```

```
$ redis-server --port 5001 --cluster-enabled yes --cluster-config-file
nodes-5001.conf --cluster-node-timeout 2000 --cluster-slave-validity-
factor 10 --cluster-migration-barrier 1 --cluster-require-full-coverage
yes --dbfilename dump-5001.rdb --daemonize yes
```

```
$ redis-server --port 5002 --cluster-enabled yes --cluster-config-file
nodes-5002.conf --cluster-node-timeout 2000 --cluster-slave-validity-
factor 10 --cluster-migration-barrier 1 --cluster-require-full-coverage
yes --dbfilename dump-5002.rdb --daemonize yes
```

The cluster is not ready to run yet. We can check the cluster's health with the **CLUSTER INFO** command:

```
$ redis-cli -c -p 5000
127.0.0.1:5000> CLUSTER INFO
cluster_state:fail
cluster_slots_assigned:0
cluster_slots_ok:0
cluster_slots_pfail:0
cluster_slots_fail:0
cluster_known_nodes:1
cluster_size:0
cluster_current_epoch:0
cluster_my_epoch:0
cluster_stats_messages_sent:0
cluster_stats_messages_received:0
127.0.0.1:5000> SET foo bar
(error) CLUSTERDOWN The cluster is down
```

The output of **CLUSTER INFO** tells us that the cluster only knows about one node (the connected node), no slots are assigned to any of the nodes, and the cluster state is *fail*.

When the cluster is in the *fail* state, it cannot process any queries, as we could see when we tried to execute the **SET** command.

Next, the 16,384 hash slots are distributed evenly across the three instances. The configuration **cluster-require-full-coverage** is set to **yes**, which means that the cluster can process queries only if all hash slots are assigned to running instances:

```
$ redis-cli -c -p 5000 CLUSTER ADDSLOTS {0..5460}
$ redis-cli -c -p 5001 CLUSTER ADDSLOTS {5461..10922}
$ redis-cli -c -p 5002 CLUSTER ADDSLOTS {10923..16383}
```

The preceding shell lines use a range trick to expand the numbers. They take the starting number and the ending number and expand them into separate numbers. It is the same as passing 0, 1, 2, 3, 4, 5, and so on up to *5460* to the first line.

The **CLUSTER ADDSLOTS** command informs the node what slots it should own. If a hash slot is already assigned, this command fails. It is possible to assign slots one by one; it does not need to be a sequence of numbers.

At this point, the hash slots are distributed evenly across the nodes, but the cluster is not ready yet. The cluster nodes still do not know about each other.

In Redis Cluster, there is a concept called **configuration epoch**, which is a number that represents the cluster state at a particular point in time.

This number is used when new events occur and the nodes need to agree on what is going to happen next (such as failover or resharding of hash slots).

When a cluster is initially created, the configuration epoch is set to *0* for each master. We can change this to help Redis start the cluster in a safe way. This is the only time when the configuration epoch should be changed manually. Redis Cluster automatically changes the configuration after it is up and running:

```
$ redis-cli -c -p 5000 CLUSTER SET-CONFIG-EPOCH 1
$ redis-cli -c -p 5001 CLUSTER SET-CONFIG-EPOCH 2
$ redis-cli -c -p 5002 CLUSTER SET-CONFIG-EPOCH 3
```

This example executes the command **CLUSTER SET-CONFIG-EPOCH** to manually set an incremental epoch to each node, which is good practice when starting a new cluster. In this example, there is no conflicting information. However, if there was conflicting information (for example, if two different nodes claimed the same hash slots), the largest epoch configuration would have priority.

Next, we are going to make all the nodes aware of each other. We will do this using the command **CLUSTER MEET**:

```
$ redis-cli -c -p 5000 CLUSTER MEET 127.0.0.1 5001
$ redis-cli -c -p 5000 CLUSTER MEET 127.0.0.1 5002
```

It is not necessary to execute **CLUSTER MEET** on each node to notify it about the existence of all the other nodes. When the first node meets the second, it means that the second node also knows about the first, and they can exchange information about other nodes that they know. When the first node meets the third node, all three nodes will know about each other eventually, through the gossip protocol that Redis Cluster implements.

Run the command **CLUSTER INFO** to see that the cluster is up and running:

```
$ redis-cli -c -p 5000
127.0.0.1:5000> CLUSTER INFO
cluster_state:ok
cluster_slots_assigned:16384
cluster_slots_ok:16384
cluster_slots_pfail:0
cluster_slots_fail:0
```

```
cluster_known_nodes:3
cluster_size:3
cluster_current_epoch:3
cluster_my_epoch:1
cluster_stats_messages_sent:164
cluster_stats_messages_received:144
127.0.0.1:5000> SET hello world
OK
```

As you can see, **CLUSTER INFO** reports that the cluster state is *ok*, all 16,384 hash slots are assigned, the current configuration epoch is 3, and the cluster knows about three nodes.

Adding slaves/replicas

There are three master nodes but no slaves. Thus, no data is replicated anywhere. This is not very safe. Data can be lost, and if any master has issues, the entire cluster will be unavailable (**cluster-require-full-coverage** is set to **yes**).

A new slave/replica can be added to the cluster by:

- Creating a new Redis instance in cluster mode
- Introducing it to the current cluster using the command **CLUSTER MEET**
- Getting the node ID of the master that will be replicated using the command **CLUSTER NODES**
- Executing the command **CLUSTER REPLICATE** to replicate a given node

Create a new Redis instance in cluster mode:

```
$ redis-server --port 5003 --cluster-enabled yes --cluster-config-file
nodes-5003.conf --cluster-node-timeout 2000 --cluster-slave-validity-
factor 10 --cluster-migration-barrier 1 --cluster-require-full-coverage
yes --dbfilename dump-5003.rdb --daemonize yes
```

Introduce it to the current cluster using the command **CLUSTER MEET**:

```
$ redis-cli -c -p 5003 CLUSTER MEET 127.0.0.1 5000
```

Get the node ID of the master that is going to be replicated by using the command **CLUSTER NODES**:

```
$ redis-cli -c -p 5003 CLUSTER NODES
b5354de29d7ec02e64580658d3f59422cfeda916 127.0.0.1:5002 master - 0
1432276450590 3 connected 10923-16383
```

```
08cbbb4c05ec977af9c4925834a71971bbea3477 127.0.0.1:5003 myself,master - 0
0 0 connected
68af8b5f533abae1888312a2fecd7cbe4ac77e0a 127.0.0.1:5001 master - 0
1432276449782 2 connected 5461-10922
f5940c6bcd6f06abb07f7d480b16630b6a597424 127.0.0.1:5000 master - 0
1432276449782 1 connected 0-5460
```

The command **CLUSTER NODES** outputs a list with all the nodes that belong to the cluster, along with their properties. Every line follows this format: *<node-id>* *<ip:port>* *<flags>* *<master>* *<ping-sent>* *<pong-recv>* *<config-epoch>* *<link-state>* *<slots>*.

For the sake of this example, we are not going to explain what each property means. We strongly recommend that you check out the Redis documentation to obtain more information.

Let's replicate the instance running on port *5000*. The output shows that the node ID for this instance is *f5940c6bcd6f06abb07f7d480b16630b6a597424*.

Since the node ID is generated randomly using */dev/urandom*, all **CLUSTER NODES** outputs in our examples are merely for demonstration.

Execute the command **CLUSTER REPLICATE** to replicate a given node:

```
$ redis-cli -c -p 5003 CLUSTER REPLICATE
f5940c6bcd6f06abb07f7d480b16630b6a597424
```

The replica is ready and **CLUSTER NODES** can confirm this:

```
$ redis-cli -c -p 5003 CLUSTER NODES
b5354de29d7ec02e64580658d3f59422cfeda916 127.0.0.1:5002 master - 0
1432276452608 3 connected 10923-16383
08cbbb4c05ec977af9c4925834a71971bbea3477 127.0.0.1:5003 myself,slave
f5940c6bcd6f06abb07f7d480b16630b6a597424 0 0 0 connected
68af8b5f533abae1888312a2fecd7cbe4ac77e0a 127.0.0.1:5001 master - 0
1432276452608 2 connected 5461-10922
f5940c6bcd6f06abb07f7d480b16630b6a597424 127.0.0.1:5000 master - 0
1432276451800 1 connected 0-5460
```

The first output line is the slave information. It said *myself,master* previously, and after **CLUSTER REPLICATE**, it became *myself,slave*.

Scaling reads using slave nodes

In order to scale Redis Cluster reads, it is possible to connect to a slave and enter read-only mode through the command **READONLY**. When a slave is in read-only mode, it does not redirect the queries that it is capable of serving. It will only redirect those queries that it is not able to serve. The only drawback of this mode is that it is possible to read stale data.

It is possible to end read-only mode with the command **READWRITE**.

It may be a good idea to use read-only mode based on the needs of the application. If read-only mode is not used, all queries will route to the master nodes. In this scenario, the master nodes could become a bottleneck, while the slaves may be idle most of the time.

Adding nodes

When a new node is added to a cluster, it is considered as a master with zero hash slots. Any client that connects to such a node and executes any query will be redirected to a different node. A master with zero slots cannot store any keys. In this section, we are going to see how to perform a reshard operation in a cluster, which means moving one or multiple hash slots from a source node to a destination node and migrating all existing keys to those slots.

In order to add a new, fully functional node to the cluster, we need to perform the following steps:

1. Create a new Redis instance in cluster mode.

2. Introduce the node to the cluster (**CLUSTER MEET**).

3. Find the node IDs of the new node and the destination node (**CLUSTER NODES**).

4. Reshard the hash slots and move the existing keys (the **CLUSTER SETSLOT** and **MIGRATE** commands).

Now, let's start performing the preceding steps:

1. Create a new Redis instance in cluster mode:

```
$ redis-server --port 6000 --cluster-enabled yes --cluster-
config-file nodes-6000.conf --cluster-node-timeout 2000 --cluster-
slave-validity-factor 10 --cluster-migration-barrier 1 --cluster-
require-full-coverage yes --dbfilename dump-6000.rdb --daemonize
yes
```

2. Introduce the node to the cluster:

```
$ redis-cli -c -p 6000 CLUSTER MEET 127.0.0.1 5000
```

3. Find the node IDs of the new node and the destination node:

```
$ redis-cli -c -p 6000 CLUSTER NODES
f5940c6bcd6f06abb07f7d480b16630b6a597424 127.0.0.1:5000 master - 0
1432276457644 1 connected 0-5460
68af8b5f533abae1888312a2fecd7cbe4ac77e0a 127.0.0.1:5001 master - 0
1432276457141 2 connected 5461-10922
08cbbb4c05ec977af9c4925834a71971bbea3477 127.0.0.1:5003 slave
f5940c6bcd6f06abb07f7d480b16630b6a597424 0 1432276457644 1
connected
8fa297d6bce5420150b6df6d06cfd921566a0498 127.0.0.1:6000
myself,master - 0 0 0 connected
b5354de29d7ec02e64580658d3f59422cfeda916 127.0.0.1:5002 master - 0
1432276457041 3 connected 10923-16383
```

Before we perform the reshard operation, we are going to store a key to populate a hash slot:

```
$ redis-cli -c -p 6000
127.0.0.1:6000> SET book "redis essentials"
-> Redirected to slot [1337] located at 127.0.0.1:5000
```

4. Reshard the hash slots and move the existing keys.

Redis Cluster only supports resharding of one hash slot at a time. If many hash slots have to be resharded, the following procedure needs to be executed once for each hash slot:

1. Import a hash slot from a source master node.

2. Export a hash slot to a destination master node.

3. Migrate all keys in that hash slot from the source to the destination, if any.

4. Notify the nodes about the new owner of the hash slot.

The steps necessary to import and export a hash slot from one node to another require the use of the **CLUSTER SETSLOT** command. This command modifies the state of a hash slot. It is used to perform sharding operations. There are four subcommands: **IMPORTING**, **MIGRATING**, **NODE**, and **STABLE**. In order to move a hash slot from one master to another, the receiving node has to change the hash slot state to *importing*, the owner of the slot has to change the state to *migrating*, and then every node in the cluster has to be notified about the new location of that hash slot.

Let's look at the commands in detail:

○ **CLUSTER SETSLOT <hash-slot> IMPORTING <source-id>**:

This subcommand changes the hash slot state to *importing*. It must be executed at the node that is going to receive the hash slot, and the node ID of the current slot owner must be passed in.

○ **CLUSTER SETSLOT <hash-slot> MIGRATING <destination-id>**:

This subcommand changes the hash slot state to *migrating*. It is the opposite of the **IMPORTING** subcommand. It must be executed at the node that owns the hash slot, and the node ID of the new slot owner must be passed in.

○ **CLUSTER SETSLOT <hash-slot> NODE <owner-id>**:

This subcommand associates a hash slot with a node. It must be executed on the source and destination nodes. Executing it on all master nodes is also recommended to avoid wrong redirects while the propagation is taking place.

When this command is executed on the destination node, the importing state is cleared and then the configuration epoch is updated.

When it is executed on the source node, the migrating state is cleared as long as no keys exist in that slot. Otherwise, an error is thrown.

○ **CLUSTER SETSLOT <hash-slot> STABLE**:

This subcommand clears any state of a hash slot (importing or migrating). It is useful when a rollback in a resharding operation is needed.

See this demonstration of how to reshard hash slot *1337*, which contains our key *book* from the source master node running on port *5000* to the destination node running on port *6000*:

```
$ redis-cli -c -p 6000 CLUSTER SETSLOT 1337 IMPORTING
f5940c6bcd6f06abb07f7d480b16630b6a597424
$ redis-cli -c -p 5000 CLUSTER SETSLOT 1337 MIGRATING
8fa297d6bce5420150b6df6d06cfd921566a0498
```

The next step moves all the keys in slot *1337* to the node running on port *6000*. We'll also look at some commands that can be used along with this command line:

- ○ **CLUSTER COUNTKEYSINSLOT <slot>** returns the number of keys in a given slot.
- ○ **CLUSTER GETKEYSINSLOT <slot> <amount>** returns an array with key names that belong to a slot based on the amount specified.
- ○ **MIGRATE <host> <port> <key> <db> <timeout>** moves a key to a different Redis instance.

The following commands move all keys in slot 1337 to the node running on port 6000:

```
$ redis-cli -c -p 5000
127.0.0.1:5000> CLUSTER COUNTKEYSINSLOT 1337
(integer) 1
127.0.0.1:5000> CLUSTER GETKEYSINSLOT 1337 1
1) "book"
127.0.0.1:5000> MIGRATE 127.0.0.1 6000 book 0 2000
OK
```

Finally, all the nodes are notified about the new owner of the hash slot:

```
$ redis-cli -c -p 5000 CLUSTER SETSLOT 1337 NODE
8fa297d6bce5420150b6df6d06cfd921566a0498
$ redis-cli -c -p 5001 CLUSTER SETSLOT 1337 NODE
8fa297d6bce5420150b6df6d06cfd921566a0498
$ redis-cli -c -p 5002 CLUSTER SETSLOT 1337 NODE
8fa297d6bce5420150b6df6d06cfd921566a0498
$ redis-cli -c -p 6000 CLUSTER SETSLOT 1337 NODE
8fa297d6bce5420150b6df6d06cfd921566a0498
```

The new assignment can be checked with **CLUSTER NODES**:

```
$ redis-cli -c -p 6000 CLUSTER NODES
f5940c6bcd6f06abb07f7d480b16630b6a597424 127.0.0.1:5000 master - 0
1432276457644 1 connected 0-1336 1338-5460
68af8b5f533abae1888312a2fecd7cbe4ac77e0a 127.0.0.1:5001 master - 0
1432276457141 2 connected 5461-10922
08cbbb4c05ec977af9c4925834a71971bbea3477 127.0.0.1:5003 slave
f5940c6bcd6f06abb07f7d480b16630b6a597424 0 1432276457644 1
connected
8fa297d6bce5420150b6df6d06cfd921566a0498 127.0.0.1:6000
myself,master - 0 0 4 connected 1337
b5354de29d7ec02e64580658d3f59422cfeda916 127.0.0.1:5002 master - 0
1432276457041 3 connected 10923-16383
```

Removing nodes

Removing a node requires resharding of all of its hash slots to other nodes, as explained in the previous section. Then, all the nodes need to remove this node from their known list of nodes.

Removing a node from the cluster after all of its hash slots are redistributed is just a matter of running **CLUSTER FORGET <node-id>** on all nodes.

The command **CLUSTER FORGET <node-id>** needs to be executed in all master nodes (except the one being removed) in 60 seconds or less. As soon as **CLUSTER FORGET** is executed, it adds the node to a ban list. This ban list exists to avoid re-addition of the node to the cluster when nodes exchange messages. The expiration time for the ban list is 60 seconds.

Redis Cluster administration using the redis-trib tool

At this point, you should be able to create clusters, reshard data, and add and remove master nodes or replicas. This section will explain how to use **redis-trib**, a tool that Redis distributes to facilitate cluster administration.

As of now, there are no great tools for managing Redis Cluster. Although **redis-trib** is the official cluster management tool, it is still very immature. We believe that different tools will emerge soon.

The script **redis-trib** is a Ruby script that uses most of the commands that we explained in the previous sections, but its interface is much simpler to use.

The **redis-trib** interface is very straightforward. It has a few commands:

```
$ cd redis-3.0.2
$ ./src/redis-trib.rb
Usage: redis-trib <command> <options> <arguments ...>

    create          host1:port1 ... hostN:portN
                    --replicas <arg>
    check           host:port
    fix             host:port
    reshard         host:port
                    --from <arg>
                    --to <arg>
                    --slots <arg>
                    --yes
    add-node        new_host:new_port existing_host:existing_port
                    --slave
```

```
                     --master-id <arg>
del-node             host:port node_id
set-timeout          host:port milliseconds
call                 host:port command arg arg .. arg
import               host:port
                     --from <arg>
help                 (show this help)
```

For **check**, **fix**, **reshard**, **del-node**, and **set-timeout**, you can specify the host and port of any working node in the cluster.

The **redis-trib** tool will be used to create a cluster with three master nodes and one slave for each master. After that, a new master is added to the cluster, and *10* slots are resharded from the master running on port *5000* to the new master. Finally, a slave is added to the cluster. The end result is shown in this architecture:

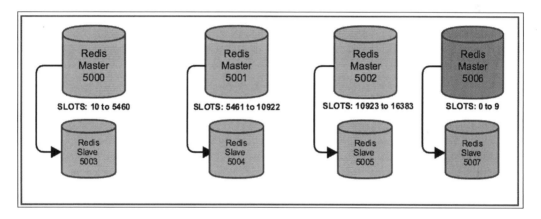

The following snippet creates eight Redis instances in cluster mode, but they are not part of a cluster yet:

```
$ for port in 5000 5001 5002 5003 5004 5005 5006 5007; do
   redis-server --port ${port} --cluster-enabled yes --cluster-config-file
nodes-${port}.conf --cluster-node-timeout 2000 --cluster-slave-validity-
factor 10 --cluster-migration-barrier 1 --cluster-require-full-coverage
yes --dbfilename dump-${port}.rdb  --daemonize yes
done
```

Create a cluster with three master nodes and one replica for each (evenly distributing the hash slots):

```
$ ./src/redis-trib.rb create --replicas 1 127.0.0.1:5000 127.0.0.1:5001
127.0.0.1:5002 127.0.0.1:5003 127.0.0.1:5004 127.0.0.1:5005
```

Add a new master node to the cluster:

```
$ ./src/redis-trib.rb add-node 127.0.0.1:5006 127.0.0.1:5000
```

Reshard 10 slots from one node to another node (run **CLUSTER NODES** to find the node IDs of the masters on ports 5000 and 5006):

```
$ ./src/redis-trib.rb reshard --from SOURCE-NODE-ID --to DESTINATION-
NODE-ID --slots 10 --yes 127.0.0.1:5000
```

Add a new slave to the cluster. The **redis-trib** tool will automatically choose the master with the least number of slaves:

```
$ ./src/redis-trib.rb add-node --slave 127.0.0.1:5007 127.0.0.1:5000
```

As you can see, managing a cluster with **redis-trib** is much easier than just using Redis commands. We presented the most important commands in **redis-trib,** but there are other commands available that you should try.

Summary

This chapter explained in detail the background of Redis Sentinel and how it works. Its goal is very simple; it is meant to provide automatic failover in a group of Redis master/slave instances, and it does not distribute data among different hosts.

Redis Cluster, on the other hand, has broader goals. It was created to make Redis a distributed data store with automatic failover and data sharding.

Different architectures were presented, along with good practices, and then cluster administration via Redis commands was shown. Lastly, **redis-trib**, a tool that makes Redis Cluster administration easier, was introduced.

The Redis website is a great source of information. It has very detailed information on all the commands available, along with many examples and specifications about Redis Cluster.

We hope you have enjoyed reading this book and learning more about the history and capabilities of Redis. We hope this book will help you the next time you have a big problem to solve using a fast key-value data store.

Index

Thank you for buying
Redis Essentials

About Packt Publishing

Packt, pronounced 'packed', published its first book, *Mastering phpMyAdmin for Effective MySQL Management*, in April 2004, and subsequently continued to specialize in publishing highly focused books on specific technologies and solutions.

Our books and publications share the experiences of your fellow IT professionals in adapting and customizing today's systems, applications, and frameworks. Our solution-based books give you the knowledge and power to customize the software and technologies you're using to get the job done. Packt books are more specific and less general than the IT books you have seen in the past. Our unique business model allows us to bring you more focused information, giving you more of what you need to know, and less of what you don't.

Packt is a modern yet unique publishing company that focuses on producing quality, cutting-edge books for communities of developers, administrators, and newbies alike. For more information, please visit our website at www.packtpub.com.

Writing for Packt

We welcome all inquiries from people who are interested in authoring. Book proposals should be sent to author@packtpub.com. If your book idea is still at an early stage and you would like to discuss it first before writing a formal book proposal, then please contact us; one of our commissioning editors will get in touch with you.

We're not just looking for published authors; if you have strong technical skills but no writing experience, our experienced editors can help you develop a writing career, or simply get some additional reward for your expertise.

Building Databases with Redis [Video]

ISBN: 978-1-78328-411-5   Duration: 03:13 hours

Acquire practical experience and skills in designing databases using Redis

1. Harness the power of the Redis to build storages as per your needs.

2. Execute Redis commands and discover ways to perform them on the database.

3. Filled with practical examples close to real-life tasks and situations.

Rapid Redis [Video]

ISBN: 978-1-78439-545-2   Duration: 00:49 hours

Get to grips with Redis; an open source, networked, in-memory, key-value data store that will solve all your storage needs

1. Understand the difference between SQL and NoSQL databases.

2. Use Redis interactively through its command-line interface (CLI).

3. Understand the basic data structures of Redis and their usage.

Please check **www.PacktPub.com** for information on our titles

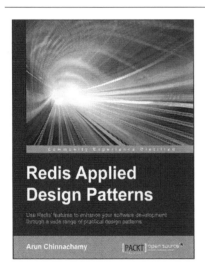

Made in the USA
San Bernardino, CA
11 April 2018